Practical Guide

FOR FIRST-YEAR TEACHERS

TEACHERS

Practical Guide
FOR FIRST-YEAR
TEACHERS

Tools for Educators
in Grades 1-3

Mary Presson Roberts

Skyhorse Publishing

First Skyhorse Publishing edition 2015.

Skyhorse Publishing books may be purchased in bulk at special discounts for sales promotion, corporate gifts, fund-raising, or educational purposes. Special editions can also be created to specifications. For details, contact the Special Sales Department, Skyhorse Publishing, 307 West 36th Street, 11th Floor, New York, NY 10018 or info@skyhorsepublishing.com.

Skyhorse® and Skyhorse Publishing® are registered trademarks of Skyhorse Publishing, Inc.®, a Delaware corporation.

Visit our website at www.skyhorsepublishing.com.

10 9 8 7 6 5 4 3 2 1

Library of Congress Cataloging-in-Publication Data is available on file.

Cover design by Michelle Lee

Print ISBN: 978-1-63220-577-3
Ebook ISBN: 978-1-63220-992-4

Printed in the United States of America

Contents

Preface

PURPOSE

Your first years of teaching can be an overwhelming experience. It is an exciting time, when you will get the opportunity to put your ideas and knowledge into practice. It is also a time when you will need much support. It is hoped that your school and school district will provide you with that needed support. If this is the case, this book will serve to supplement that support system. If you do not have a great deal of support, this book will offer many ideas and suggestions to help you in your first years of teaching.

In my first years of teaching, I did not have a great deal of support. Consequently, I wanted to find a way to use my experiences in the classroom to help others have a positive experience in the beginning of their careers. This book will be a reference covering many areas of need for beginning teachers. Some of the areas covered may not have been addressed in your teaching preparation program.

INTENDED AUDIENCE AND ANTICIPATED USES

This book is targeted to student teachers, substitute teachers, teachers new to the profession, teachers returning to the profession, emergency credential teachers, as well as those training the above-mentioned professionals. Prior to writing the book, I surveyed professionals in the above-mentioned categories to find out what they would like to see included in a teaching reference. The contents of this book have been tailored, based upon the survey results, to meet the needs of those just entering the teaching profession. This book will be a valuable reference tool for those in their first few years of teaching.

KNOWLEDGE BASE OF THE BOOK

The book is based upon my experiences teaching in the primary grades. This year I will begin my fourteenth year of teaching in the primary grades. The contents of the book are based on experience rather than on research. All of the professionals, students, and parents I have worked with have influenced the contents of this book.

OVERVIEW OF THE SCOPE AND ORGANIZATION

This book is divided into twelve chapters. These chapters focus on: classroom environment, parent communications, parent involvement, discipline, instructional planning, developing themes, instructional presentation, differentiation of instruction, student assessment and record keeping, using technology in the classroom, planning for special events, and the professionalism of teaching.

Chapter 1 guides the reader in setting up a classroom as a learning environment. Directions are given for placement of the furniture, setting up attractive student learning stations, and decorating the classroom by using teacher-made materials. A diagram of a classroom and photographs of actual classroom settings provide pictorial examples.

Chapter 2 provides the reader with descriptions and concrete examples of strong parent communications. The Beginning of the Year Letter, weekly newsletter, and Open House newsletter have been described in detail. Following the descriptions, actual newsletters used for a primary classroom have been provided. Suggestions for creating a video to be shown to parents during Open House have also been provided.

The chapter goes on to give helpful hints about scheduling, preparing for, and conducting parent-teacher conferences. A sample form for scheduling conferences is included. Two sample conference reports, to be filled out by the teacher prior to each conference, have been completed for reference.

The chapter concludes by giving information regarding how to handle phone and written communications between home and school. It also gives tips for bridging the communication gap with hard-to-reach families.

Chapter 3 gives easy ways to get parents involved in classroom activities with minimal teacher preparation. The chapter describes how to recruit and use parents as tutors for students requiring additional support. Suggestions are given to invite parents to be guest speakers to share their own knowledge, read stories to the class, serve as lunch buddies for students, and serve as chaperons on class trips. Advice for dealing with conflicts with parents is also given in this chapter.

In Chapter 4 the importance of strong classroom discipline is discussed. The chapter begins with a section about rules and consequences. A positive and negative chart management system is explained and depicted in a photograph. The importance of providing a highly structured classroom environment and being prepared as a teacher to prevent discipline problems is discussed.

Methods to document behaviors inconsistent with the classroom plan are given through examples of a documentation log and sample daily student checklists.

The first section of Chapter 5 deals with how to create long-range plans for the entire year. A long-range plan for a primary classroom is given as an example. This long-range plan lists themes of study, books to be used for each theme, and major skills that will be covered through each theme. Illustrations of student projects relating to the themes appear throughout this section.

The next section of the chapter focuses on short-range planning. This refers to completion of lesson plans. Sample lesson plans, as they would appear in a lesson plan book, have been given for one week.

Good practices for working with members of a grade-level planning team are given. A sample of a team planning form is given as a way to ensure all members of the planning team work to do their share of the planning and come to the planning sessions prepared.

Guidelines are explained for leaving meaningful plans and activities for a substitute teacher. A sample lesson plan for a substitute teacher is included. Emergency lesson plans are described.

Many examples and ideas are given for planning for the first day of school, planning for the typical day of school, and planning for the end of the school year. Activities for the first day of school are described in sequential order. These activities include instructional as well as management activities. A typical day for an early elementary classroom has been planned using times of the day as reference. This plan shows what types of activities should be planned for each day and the approximate amount of time the activities should take. Discussing the end of the year, several fun activities are described that will benefit the teacher, the students, and the parents.

Chapter 6 discusses how to develop themes and gather materials for themes on a budget. Eleven extensive lesson plans are given for the theme of weather. Photographs, worksheets, and other visuals accompany the lesson plans. A bibliography of fiction, nonfiction, and poetry selections is also given for the theme of weather.

Chapter 7 describes what should be included in an instructional presentation. The instructional presentation has been broken up into its components: beginning, middle, and ending. After descriptions of what should be included in the beginning, middle, and ending of each lesson, a sample math lesson for a primary class is broken down into these components.

Chapter 8 focuses on the importance of differentiating instruction and instructional activities within the classroom to meet the needs of all students. Suggestions and examples are given for differentiating by layering student assignments, using grouping strategies, and using student work centers.

Chapter 9 focuses on five aspects of student assessment and record keeping. Explanations are given regarding creating student portfolios, setting up and maintaining grade books, completing report cards, grading daily class work, and grading homework.

The tremendous impact of technology in the classroom is discussed in Chapter 10. Suggestions are given for using the computer as a communication tool, as a tool for developing instructional activities for students, and as an avenue for students to learn and to practice skills to enhance the instructional program. Advice is also given for use of photography in the classroom.

Chapter 11 describes how to plan for, recruit volunteers for, and properly supervise classroom parties and field trips.

Two types of classroom parties are described. Things that need to be done by the teacher to prepare for classroom parties are listed. Management tips to be used during the course of the party are given.

Guidelines for teacher responsibilities before and during a field trip are highlighted. Effectively recruiting and using parent volunteers is described. Procedures are given to ensure a positive field trip experience for all participants.

Chapter 12 focuses on maintaining professionalism and growing as a professional. This begins with relationships with students, parents, colleagues, and administrators. Advice is given for making these relationships positive and professional.

The importance of getting involved in school committees and professional organizations is discussed. What teachers can gain through participation in these organizations is explained.

Creating and maintaining a professional portfolio is recommended. Ideas for what to include in a professional portfolio are listed. Uses for professional portfolios are also discussed.

ACKNOWLEDGMENTS

I would like to thank those who have helped me prior to and throughout my teaching career to shape the kind of teacher I have become. These include: All of my colleagues, students, parents, and administrators at Jane Edwards Elementary School (Edisto Island, South Carolina), Oakland Elementary School (Charleston, South Carolina), and Selwyn Elementary School (Charlotte, North Carolina). Very special thanks to Alverta Bowens for giving me my first teaching position, to Richard Cancro and Dot Williams for being my mentors, and to Joyce King, Brenda White, Gwyn Kellam, Ellyn Clifford, Becky Garagiola, and Julia Marshall for being daily supporters at these schools. Thanks to my professors at Winthrop University (Rock Hill, South Carolina) and The Citadel (Charleston, South Carolina) for such fine educational experiences and continued support. Thanks to Stormy Young (Fort Mill, South Carolina) for providing himself as a role model of what a real teacher is and does for children.

Thanks to my fellow educators and friends Tanji Coats and Cindy Fisk for their help with this project as well as for their true and lasting friendship.

Special thanks to Nance Presson for the beautiful line illustrations for pp. 2, 4, 5, 8, 11, 12, 13, 16, 17, 18, 19, 21, 22, 23, 49, 50, 66, 91, 106, 109, 120, 122, and 138. Thanks also to my fabulous student line illustrators: Carey Carpenter (pp. 7, 24, 25, 53, 61, 149), Emily Carpenter (p. 52), and Laura Carpenter (pp. 7, 64, 149). Thanks also to their partents, Jody and Beth Carpenter

I would like to thank my family for their support with this project and all that has led up to it. I couldn't have done it without them. Extra special thanks to my mother, Nance Presson, who never doubted that I could do it.

Appreciative acknowledgment is made to the following individuals and companies for permission to use their materials in this book:

Barry Bosher
Lee Canter and Marlene Canter
Carey Carpenter, Emily Carpenter, and Laura Carpenter
Charlotte-Mecklenburg School District
Creative Teaching Press
Dixon Ticonderoga Company
Ellison Educational Equipment, Inc.
Julia Marshall
Marvy
Punkydoodles
Scholastic, Inc.
Jerry Stone, PPNC
Liza Wooten
The Wright Group

The contributions of the following reviewers are gratefully acknowledged:

Sheila Martin
Teacher
Trinity Lutheran Preschool and Kindergarten
Potter, KS

Anita Perry
Elementary Teacher,
Leominster School District
Leominster, MA

Barbara Foulks-Boyd
Professor of Education
Radford University
Radford, VA

Debbie Wilks
Third-Grade Teacher
Riverside Culture Arts and History Magnet School
Wichita, KS

Joan Commons
Academic Coordinator, Teacher Education
CREATE Project
University of California
San Diego, CA

Rachael Hungerford
Assistant Professor of Education
Department Chair
Lycoming College
Williamsport, PA

About the Author

Mary Presson Roberts currently teaches first grade for the Charlotte-Mecklenburg School District. She has taught primary grades in three different schools for 13 years. Working with children in schools located in Edisto Island, South Carolina; Charleston, South Carolina; and Charlotte, North Carolina has given her the opportunity to work with children of different backgrounds and socioeconomic groups.

She received her Bachelor's Degree in Elementary Education from Winthrop University, Rock Hill, South Carolina in 1987. She received her Master's Degree in School Administration from The Citadel, Charleston, South Carolina in 1995, where she graduated with distinction.

In her 13 years in the educational profession, Mary Presson Roberts has served as Teaching Assistant Principal and Grade Level Chairperson. She has also served as a representative on grant writing committees and on a school-based management team, teacher advisory council, school improvement committee, writing committee, and social committee.

Introduction

I don't think any teacher will forget his or her first days of teaching. No matter how well trained we are, or how fantastic our methods courses or student teaching experiences have been, the sheer terror experienced when seeing our first students and knowing we are on our own is indescribable.

I hope that your first years of teaching will be in an ideal place where those possessing much more knowledge than you will extend their support. Many schools and school districts offer tremendous support systems for new teachers, such as one-to-one mentoring programs and discussion groups. Unfortunately, this is not always the case for the novice teacher.

My first 2 years of teaching were in a school on an island off the coast of South Carolina. I had a second-grade position. It would have been wonderful if I had had as a resource a strong, experienced, second-grade teacher to advise me during that first year. As it was, I was the most experienced teacher in the second grade because there was only one second-grade class. Not only was this a challenge, but the first-, third-, and fourth-grade teachers were also brand new teachers. This school's isolated location created difficulties attracting and keeping more seasoned teachers. All of the teachers at this school would have benefited from a resource like this book.

To my first position I brought enthusiasm, a philosophy of education, a great need to change the world, a few construction paper room decorations, and little else. I would have thrived under the guidance of an experienced teacher next door. Unfortunately, being taken under an experienced teacher's wing is not always possible.

For those of you about to enter the teaching profession, just entering the teaching profession, seasoned teachers looking for new ideas, or teachers reentering the teaching profession, I hope this book will be a mentoring tool.

Teaching touches so many lives. So far, in my teaching career, I have taught primary students in both North and South Carolina. I have taught an average of 23 students per year. In 13 years, I have worked directly with at least 299 young people. I hope that I have made a positive impact on their lives.

In my teaching experiences and positions, I received students who benefited from mandatory kindergarten experiences. Several references to kindergarten have been made in this book. I also have worked in school districts where I have had to accompany children and supervise them during lunch and recess each day. References have been made to this effect.

This book provides recommendations based upon my experiences in the educational field. Throughout your career you will find things that you will use forever. Other things you might use for only a short period of time. All of your knowledge and experiences will work together to create your unique teaching style and experience.

Good teachers are good learners. Excellent teachers always strive to learn to perfect their teaching. You will need to use as many resources as possible in your career to make sure that the imprint you leave on children is a positive one that will instill in them the gift of loving learning.

1

Classroom Environment

Before the year begins, you will need to set up your classroom as a learning environment. It is very important to provide an attractive, stimulating, colorful environment for your students to learn in. Often, parents and students will gain a first impression of a teacher by what they see upon entering the classroom. Create a positive first impression by carefully arranging your furniture, setting up attractive student learning centers, and decorating with creative and meaningful items.

Think carefully about the way the furniture in your room is arranged. You will need to make sure you have comfortable areas for student seating, a common meeting area on the carpet, an area for reading group and other small group work, and learning center stations. It may be helpful to work this out using drawings before you actually start moving furniture. You could then cut out paper to the size of each piece of furniture and arrange the paper according to your drawings. It is much easier to move pieces of paper than it is to move heavy pieces of furniture.

For student seating, primary students often work well at tables with other students. If you do not have tables for student seating, you can arrange your desks into table-like clusters. For example, if you are going to have 25 students, you can arrange your desks into five groups of five. This type of arrangement allows students to get to know one another, work cooperatively, and work to share supplies and materials. It also promotes a community-type atmosphere.

Once you have arranged your tables or desks, you will need to decide, prior to the arrival of the students, where each student will sit. Look carefully at your class list to make sure your tables have equity of gender and race. If your students attended your school last year, go to see the students' previous teachers to determine if any of your students have special needs that should be addressed when considering seating. Label each student desk by placing a nameplate on the desk. For the first few weeks of school, you will need to make the names temporary since not all of the students on your roll will actually show up, and some students may go by names other than the ones you were given. Attractive nameplates can be purchased at teaching supply stores or you can use sentence strips. Your school may supply sentence strips. You may also wish to add an alphabet strip or number line atop each student desk. A simple way to adhere these items to tables and desks is to cover nameplates, alphabets, and number lines with a large piece of clear contact paper. The contact paper will come off the desks when you need to remove it.

On top of each table, place a basket of books and a basket to store supplies in. Students will use the books throughout the year to read when they have completed their class work. This will be the students' signal to you that they are finished with their work and ready for another activity or to go to a learning center. Make sure to change the books in the baskets frequently. The books in each basket should represent a variety of interests, genres, and reading levels. If teaching thematically, you may wish to place theme-related books in the book baskets. You may also want to place additional materials such as math games, manipulatives, folder games, and so on, into these baskets. Supply baskets should contain the supplies students will use every day. The baskets should contain scissors, glue, crayons, and pencils. When choosing your baskets or tubs for supplies and books, keep in mind the purpose of each container and look for durability.

You will need an area of the room, especially for primary students, where all students can be seated comfortably on the floor. You will use this area for sharing books and conducting whole group instruction. Many times, younger students have difficulties selecting and sitting in their own personal spaces. You may wish to put pieces of tape down on the floor or carpet to mark each child's individual space. Once you get to know your students, you may even wish to assign each student a regular personal space in this common area. This can easily be achieved by labeling each piece of tape with a student's name. Throughout the year, places on the community area should be changed to give students who have had to sit farthest from you a closer spot or to put students next to people whom they will best work alongside.

Choose one or two spaces in the room for group work. These spaces will be where you conduct your small group instruction. A table with chairs for all students participating in the group is ideal. If possible, this area should be free for your use at all times. If you have a teaching assistant, you will want two areas so you and your assistant can work with groups simultaneously. If two groups are going on at one time, you will want these stations far enough apart so that activities in one area do not distract from the other. Both quiet and more active center stations should be placed some distance away from the group work areas as well.

Use the perimeter of the classroom for learning center stations. If possible, make five center areas to provide a variety of choices for your students. Center areas should be able to accommodate two or three students at a time. As examples, you may have a listening station, a writing center, a science center, a math center, and a language arts center. Center spaces should have enough room for students to work with hands-on activities and materials.

After your room has been arranged physically, it is time to decorate. Decorating can be done inexpensively. Before you decorate, make sure you check your school's policies regarding what type of adhesives can be used, fire laws, whether materials can hang from the ceiling, whether murals can be painted, and so on.

Many of your classroom decorations should be tied in to your students' learning objectives. For example, in a first-grade classroom, decorations might be used to display the days of the week, months of the year, alphabet, calendar, and number line. This classroom might have the days of the week printed on different types of dinosaurs. The months of the year might be displayed on cars of a train. Decorative alphabets, calendars, and number lines can be purchased commercially or handmade.

To make decorations, find outlines of shapes and things that will appeal to your students. You may find things that are of particular interest in your region or for that specific year. The pictures you select can then be enlarged to the size you want using a copying machine. Once you have arrived at the size you want, make copies of the shapes on colorful paper. Laminate for durability. After you laminate items, write whatever information you want to display on them using a permanent marker. Writing on the shapes after you have laminated them will enable you to

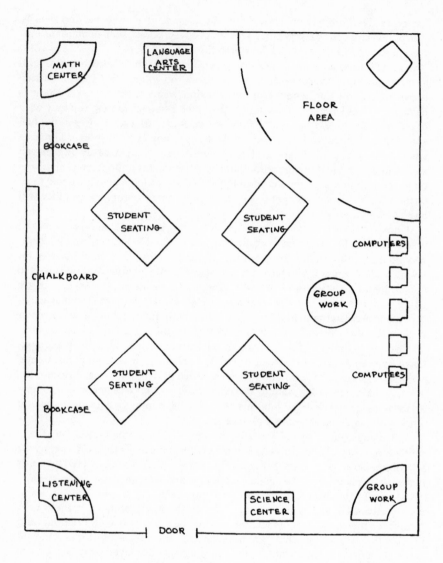

remove the writing if you wish. By using rubbing alcohol or fingernail polish remover, you can wipe permanent marker off of laminated materials.

Often, beginning teachers are on a very tight budget. Most classroom decorations need to be handmade rather than store-bought for this reason. Following are some decorating ideas for teachers on a tight budget:

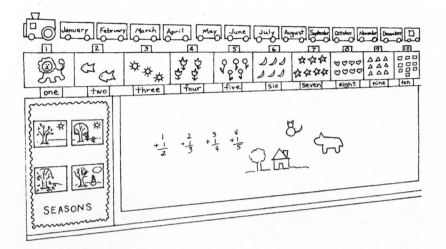

- If your classroom's paint is old and peeling, ask your principal if he of she would supply paint so that you can paint the classroom yourself to suit your needs.
- Use laminated magazine pictures of animals, plants, and other appealing things to make a collage on one wall or area of wall in your classroom. This collage can be used throughout the year for writing assignments, discussions, and more.
- Use recommended, grade-level sight or vocabulary words to make word mobiles. Write words on index cards. Glue index cards on the fronts and backs of colorful paper. Laminate all cards. Once the cards have been laminated, string them together with ribbon or yarn. Hang the mobiles along an area of the room.
- Laminate book jackets of children's books. Display these attractive book jackets with a catchy heading. For example: "Go anywhere . . . Read!"
- Use hanging, clear plastic shoe containers to make mail slots for students. On the first day of school, use an instant camera to take pictures of each of your students. Staple each child's picture inside a plastic pocket. Students can receive mail throughout the school year in their slots.
- Create a bulletin board background that can remain the same all year. Simply cover the bulletin board with paper and border. Use this bulletin board throughout the school year to display students' work. You may want to place a slogan such as "Look Closely to See What We Have Been Doing" at the top of the bulletin board. For this slogan, you may also wish to add a magnifying glass cutout. As the year goes on, display different types of work completed by your students on the bulletin board to reflect the different types of things your students are doing in class.

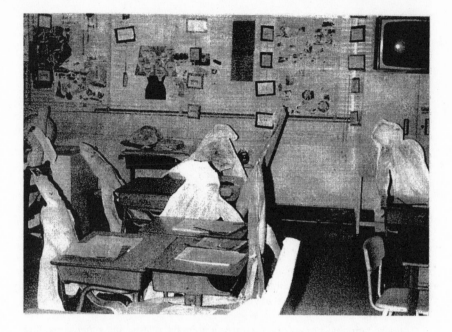

Keep in mind, when you are decorating your classroom and creating bulletin boards, to leave plenty of spaces in the room to display students' work. By far the best decorations are those created by the students. Students get a real boost from seeing their work displayed in the classroom. Always be sure to include pieces from each student somewhere in the room. Students feel ownership of the classroom if their work is regularly highlighted. Parents visiting the classroom will be much more interested in looking for their child's work on your walls than seeing the newest bulletin board kit from the local teaching supply store.

Your classroom should reflect your students' personalities and talents, and the things being covered academically. Those entering your classroom should see evidence of the creative and meaningful learning occurring within. Pages 7 and 8 show representative pieces of student art.

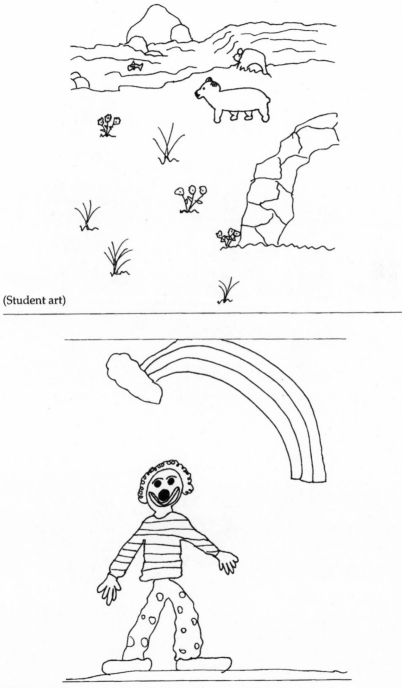

(Student art)

(Student art)

2

Parent Communications

Strong communication between school and parents regarding what is going on in your classroom is an essential element contributing to your success and that of your students. Parents are much more likely to be supportive of you and your program if they are kept well informed and feel that their input is valued. This section will focus on written communications, phone communications, and conferencing techniques. Dealing with families with difficulties communicating with the school will also be addressed. Many concrete examples are provided.

BEGINNING OF THE YEAR LETTER

Your Beginning of the Year Letter will give parents basic information about you and your program. This will be the first written communication the parents receive from you and their first impression of you. It is always essential that your written communications are free of spelling and grammatical errors. If you are using a computer, always use the spell check feature. Also, always have someone proofread all your written communications prior to sending them home. Often there are things the computer will not catch that one of your colleagues will.

Begin your first letter by letting the parents know something about you. Include your training, experience, and outside interests. Parents are interested in your qualifications as well as you as a person.

The Beginning of the Year Letter should give a brief philosophy of your approach to teaching and learning. Give an explanation of how you plan to help the students learn the subject matter. If you teach thematically, let the parents know what that means. Be careful not to get bogged down in teacher jargon that will not be understood by the parents. Keep in mind that the parents have not been introduced to many terms educators frequently use. Also, educational terms change often.

A section in your Beginning of the Year Letter should be devoted to your behavioral expectations of the students. State why it is so important that high expectations will be necessary to provide the excellent educational climate that all students deserve. In this section, list your rules for behavior, positive consequences for following the rules, negative consequences for rule infractions, and methods of communicating rules and consequences to students. For example, if you use positive and negative chart systems in your classroom, explain and show exactly how you use the chart system.

The next section of the newsletter can explain how you will communicate with the parents throughout the year. This would be the time to mention that parents will receive a weekly (or bimonthly or monthly) newsletter highlighting the events and curriculum being covered in the classroom each week. Also give information regarding how often parents will receive graded classroom work, progress reports, report cards, and so on.

The grading policy for your classroom, in alignment with your district, could be included in your Beginning of the Year Letter. This will enable your parents to understand the grades on work sent home for review.

Your expectations for homework completion should also be included. Let parents know when to expect homework assignments, how much time the average homework assignment will take, how much parental assistance should be given, and whether homework assignments will be for extra practice of material already covered or for enrichment purposes. Based on my experience, primary students should spend no more than 30 to 40 minutes per school night on homework. Half of this time should be spent reading. A reading record can be sent home each school night. In the reading record, parents should fill out the date, the title of the book or books read, and sign their name(s). The purpose of all homework completion in the early primary grades should be one of encouraging responsibility and setting the groundwork for good study habits while reinforcing work that is being done at school. Unless parents specifically request weekend homework, homework should not be assigned over the weekends.

Here is an example of a Beginning of the Year Letter I sent home to my first-graders. Many of the elements described above have been included in this letter. I also added other information I felt necessary to communicate with my students' parents at the beginning of the year.

Welcome to Mrs. Roberts's First-Grade Class!

Dear Parents,

It is with great enthusiasm that I welcome you and your child to first grade. I am looking forward to working with you throughout this exciting and rewarding first-grade year.

This is my eighth year teaching first grade at ABC Elementary School and my thirteenth year teaching primary education. I received my Bachelor's Degree in Elementary Education at Winthrop University. I recently earned my Master's Degree in School Administration from The Citadel.

Please feel free at any time during the school year to communicate with me regarding your child's progress.

In order to provide our students with the optimal educational climate they deserve, we will observe the following school and classroom rules:

School and Classroom Rules

1. Follow directions.

2. Respect all adults, students, and property.

3. Keep hands, feet, and objects to yourself.

4. Walk, do not run.

5. Raise your hand.

School and classroom rules will be communicated thoroughly to the students.

Positive and negative consequences for behaviors will be used in the classroom.

Students will receive hole punches in cards for demonstrating positive behaviors. At the end of the week, students who have five or more hole punches will get to participate in a special activity. The student or students receiving the most hole punches in a given week will receive a Student-of-the-Week Award.

Positive Consequences

1. Individual Rewards

    a. End-of-the-week activity

    b. Treasure Chest

    c. Student-of-the-Week Award

2. Class Rewards

    a. Class Parties

    b. Extra Center Time

    c. Class Snacks

Negative Consequences

Different colored tags will be used on the chart to indicate rule infractions. At the beginning of each day, students will begin with a green tag. If a tag is turned to yellow, it indicates a warning to the student. Following yellow, red tags will be used.

1 red tag   = loss of 5 minutes
                  recess time
2 red tags = loss of all recess time
3 red tags = parent is contacted
4 red tags = office referral

Supplies

The following is the first-grade supply list. Please send these supplies to school with your child as soon as possible.

- 24 pencils
- white glue
- book bag
- 3 sewn composition books
- 2 boxes of facial tissue
- 1 bottle of antibacterial hand soap
- 1 pack of markers
- 1 pack of colored pencils

Please feel free to contact me if you have difficulty getting these supplies.

Supplies will be collected when they are brought to school and will be distributed as needed. Supplies will be placed on tables each day for student use. Years of experience have shown me that this is the best way to make sure all children have the needed supplies for each school day.

Donations of plastic sandwich bags, instant film, sponges, and baby wipes would be greatly appreciated.

Special Classes

Following are the special classes your child will attend each week. This schedule is to help you get your child ready each day. For example, please make sure your child has on suitable attire for physical education and brings his or her library book on days attending Media.

Monday	9:00-9:30	Music
Tuesday	9:00-9:45	Art
Thursday	9:00-9:45	Media
Friday	9:00-9:30	P.E.

Daily Schedule for Students

7:15 First buses arrive. Breakfast is available in the cafeteria.

7:50 Tardy bell for homeroom rings.

11:30 Lunch

1:00 Recess

2:00 Bus students are escorted to the buses.

2:10 Walkers, car riders, and children attending the after school program are dismissed.

NOTE: The above discipline plan was adapted from *Assertive Discipline: Positive Behavior Management For Today's Classroom*, 1992, by Lee Canter and Marlene Canter.

Student Work for Your Review

A packet of your child's work will be sent home twice a month for your review. You will be able to go over the work with your child and then keep the work sent home. You will sign the envelope the work was sent in and return it to school the next day. A space will be provided on the envelope for comments.

Homework

Beginning next week, homework will be assigned daily, Monday through Thursday. Completion of homework is a very important aspect of the academic process. Homework not only reinforces work done at school, it also gives you the opportunity to be involved in your child's education. Homework also promotes responsibility and good study habits in young children. Homework assignments must be signed by a parent or guardian and returned to school the next day. Your child will lose a portion of recess if his or her homework assignments are not completed and signed.

Snack

There will be no organized classroom daily snack. However, if you would like your child to have a daily snack, simply send one each day for your child to eat on the playground during the afternoon recess.

At the Open House meeting planned for September, I will be asking for volunteers to provide snacks for the class for our end-of-the-week activities.

Communications

Communication between home and school is a key to your child's success! Each week you will receive a newsletter highlighting the events and activities planned for that week.

Any time you have questions regarding your child and his or her progress, please send a note to school with your child or call the office to leave a message for me. I will get back in touch with you as soon as possible.

I am also available to meet with you to discuss concerns in the mornings before students arrive or in the afternoons following student dismissal. Let me know if you would like to schedule a conference.

By working together as a team, I am confident that we will make this an excellent, rewarding first-grade year!

Sincerely,

Mary P. Roberts

WEEKLY NEWSLETTER

The weekly newsletter will be one of your most valuable tools of communication. Through the weekly newsletter, parents will be informed about the curriculum being covered, the materials being used, and your methods of teaching the subject matter. The time spent each week on your newsletter will become invaluable and save you time in the long run. You will save time by answering ahead of time questions parents might have. This will cut down on the number of letters, phone calls, and conferences you will have to have.

Begin your newsletter each week by letting the parents know what theme or major course of study you will be working with and for what period of time. If you are teaching thematically, let the parents know what the broad theme will be and how many weeks you will be working on this theme. The majority of the remainder of the newsletter should show how you plan to cover each of the academic subjects under the main theme.

A section should be devoted to language arts. You may wish to include literature selections that you will be using in the classroom that week. Also, list specific skills that will be taught with these literature selections. If you are using reading groups in the classroom, specify which stories and skills will be covered in your reading groups.

Following the literature section, a section on phonetic focus is helpful. Each week, list major phonetic elements and skills that will be covered. In this section, you may wish to include and incorporate your spelling list. For example:

This week we will be working with the **short a** vowel sound. This is the sound the letter **a** makes in the words **cat, apple, man,** and **sad.** Our spelling words for the week all have the **short a** sound. Spelling words for the week will be:

Pattern words	1.	man
	2.	can
	3.	ran
	4.	tan
	5.	pan
	6.	van
Challenge words	7.	apple
	8.	alligator

Another major section of the newsletter should be devoted to your math program. List the mathematical objectives that you will be working toward during the week. You may also wish to explain how these objectives will be achieved. For example:

> This week we will be working with addition and subtraction facts with sums to 18. We will be using a variety of strategies that will move students from the concrete level to the symbolic level. Use of cubes, counting on, and number lines will be strategies used to assist students with this skill. We will also be reviewing two- and three-dimensional shapes this week.

The next section of the newsletter should address skills, concepts, and experiments that will be conducted in science, health, and social studies. For example:

> This week we will be learning the differences between living and nonliving things. Students will make shadowboxes depicting living and nonliving things using magazine pictures, items found on the nature trail, and items found in the classroom.

The final portion of your newsletter could highlight upcoming events, requests for needed supplies, thank you notes to helpful parents, and recognition of special students.

Work with the newsletter format and find what is comfortable for you. The newsletter can be done on the computer using any newsletter program. There are many programs that have educational clip art that you may want to use. If you do not have access to a computer, the newsletter can be handwritten. You may wish to add graphics or borders to your newsletter. There are many border and clip art books available on the market. Or, if you are artistic, you may wish to add your own graphics and borders. Student artwork could also be used for this purpose.

However you choose to do your newsletter—how often and what day of the week you choose to send it home, what you choose to include—just keep in mind that the main purpose of this newsletter is to keep your parents informed. Use the following newsletter examples as well as newsletters done by your colleagues as a guide. Find your own style and run with it!

Mrs. Roberts's Room
News for the week of
August 24

Dear Parents,

The first week of school couldn't have gone any better! I am so pleased with the class and how quickly they have acclimated to first grade. It is going to be a fantastic school year!

I will be spending a great deal of time in the next 3 weeks assessing the students in language and mathematics. These assessments will enable me to plan small group activities that will reach each student's skill and ability level. From here, we can take your child as far as he/she can go in this first grade year by building upon the knowledge and skills he/she already possesses.

This week, the students will be working on a thematic unit titled, Back from the Beach: A School Picnic. All of the subject areas will tie into the theme. Thematic units hold the interest of the students much more so than teaching skills in isolation.

Our literature selections for the week include:

    The Picnic

    Blues #1 Picnic

    Peanut Butter and Jelly: A Play Rhyme

    The Teddy Bears' Picnic

With these selections, we will: identify rhyming words, plan a perfect picnic, write invitations, and select a favorite piece of literature and discuss what makes it appealing to the reader.

In mathematics, students will identify numerals, count items served at a picnic, and work with the number words one through ten.

Our phonics focus will be the initial consonant sounds for R, N, T, and V. We will begin the study of each letter with a poem containing many words beginning with the letter of study. We will identify words we know in the poem. We will then brainstorm words beginning with the consonant sound. These words will be put on charts and students will select words they want to write and read for reward stamps. We will then use some of the charted words to make silly sentences to write and read for stamps. Through this process, students at varying levels of reading readiness will have challenges throughout the phonics lesson.

Any time during the school year that your child will be going home in any way other than what was communicated with

me at the beginning of the year (for example, if your child will be riding home on a bus with another student or riding home in someone else's car), I will need notice of this change to be sent in writing.

If I do not have a letter letting me know of the change in transportation plans, even if the child tells me that he or she is supposed to go home in a different

way, I will have to send the child home in the usual manner. This is a school policy and in place for your child's protection.

Many thanks to Lisa's family for sending in the delicious cupcakes for our first Friday Fun activities! The children had a wonderful time. This week, for Friday Fun, we will have a picnic lunch. You will be receiving invitations and more information about our picnic tomorrow. As dessert for our picnic, it would be nice to have watermelon. Please let me know if any of you would be willing to send in individual

slices of watermelon for the children this Friday. We currently have 26 children in our class.

Please send to school any magazines that you have at home for us to use for classroom purposes. We do many magazine searches and will cut pictures and words from the magazines you send.

Beginning this evening, your child will bring home a reading record each evening. Please read with your child for 15 to 20 minutes each evening. After completing the reading, fill out the reading record with the information requested. This will be a part of your child's nightly homework. Your child may read a book from the classroom, from home, from the media center, or from the public library to fulfill nightly reading requirements.

When completing nightly reading, feel free to read books to your child, have your child read to you, or do a combination by trading off during the reading. Even as your child learns to read, it is still important to read to him or her. Your reading will demonstrate fluent reading and expose your child to materials he or she is not yet able to read on his or her own.

Have a terrific week!

Sincerely,

Mary P. Roberts

Mrs. Roberts's Room News
for the week of
September 28

Dear Parents,

This week, we will begin a unit about autumn with a special emphasis on the books of Lois Elhert. Lois Elhert's books have themes that tie nicely to autumn studies.

Literature selections for the week will include:

> *Seasons*
> *Spring, Summer, Fall, and Winter*
> *Why Do Leaves Change Color?*
> *Fresh Fall Leaves*
> *Fish Eyes*
> *Nuts to You!*

With these selections, we will recall factual information, sort leaves according to attributes, write in response to reading, and create Autumn counting books.

Students will work in reading groups this week with *The Giving Tree* and *Up in a Tree* to sequence events of a story. Students will also work to make words using the letters in "Autumn Days."

In phonics, we will be finishing our work with initial consonant and final consonant sounds.

Students will be working at their own pace this year in mathematics. Children will work in skill groups, to be introduced to mathematical concepts as they are ready. Although many math lessons will be for the entire group, those children ready to advance to higher-level skills will be given the opportunity to do so.

In our Autumn unit, we will continue our work with addition facts, problem solving, creating graphs (real, picture, and bar graphs), and making reasonable estimates.

In science, we will work to identify the parts of plants. We will use food coloring to show how plants absorb nutrients from the soil.

We will be making leaf prints this

week in class. Please send in any interestingly shaped leaves with your child for this activity. Also, please send in something your child can wear over his or her clothing as a smock to protect clothing while painting.

We greatly appreciate all of the wonderful treasure box donations that have been sent in. The children really look forward to visits to the classroom treasure box!

Have a fantastic week.

Sincerely,

Mary P. Roberts

Mrs. Roberts's Room News
for the week of
October 13

Dear Parents,

This week we will begin a Creepy Crawly unit that will extend through the next 3 weeks. Students will learn the differences between and similarities of insects and spiders. All learning activities will be based upon insects and spiders.

Literature selections for the week include:

> There's an Ant in Anthony
> Antics
> Two Bad Ants
> "I Can't," Said the Ant
> Backyard Insects
> Amazing Spiders

With these selections, we will make a chart about spiders and insects listing their names, number of legs, number of body parts, where they live, and whether or not they are poisonous. We will also work with rhyming words, write story summaries, recall factual information, and sort books into works of fiction and nonfiction.

Our phonics focus for the week will be the **short a** sound. We will begin with the book *There's an Ant in Anthony*. Students will complete an Ants in the Pants activity to sort words with **short a** and **long a** vowel sounds. The **short a** sound is the sound the letter a makes in an, cat, man, and Anthony. We will focus more extensively later on the **long a** vowel

sound (found in words such as **cake, a, may,** etc.).

Students will work with the books *I Like to Find Things*, *The Ant and the Grasshopper*, and *The Very Hungry Caterpillar* in reading groups this week.

In centers for the Creepy Crawly unit, students will make a creepy crawly character. They will attach legs to the character by deciding the beginning and ending sounds of the picture shown on the character's body part. Students will also write a story about a stamp pad spider family, decorate a butterfly and write about it, read books about Creepy Crawlies, listen to books about Creepy Crawlies, view an insect film strip, and work on the creepy crawly literature-based unit using the computer.

In science, students will compare and contrast insects and arachnids. Students will work to label the body parts of insects and arachnids.

This week, your child will begin the spelling program you received information about last week. Each week, your child will be assigned three words pertaining to a spelling pattern we are working with, three words that are sight words he or she needs to learn, and two or three challenge words. The first six words must be learned for the test each week. The challenge words are optional and it is up to you and your child whether or not your child studies these words. Challenge words spelled correctly will count as extra credit. Spelling tests will be given each Friday.

This week, your child's spelling words are:

Pattern words   1. cat
                       2. fat
                       3. hat
Sight words   4. this
                       5. that
                       6. some

Challenge words   7. insect
                           8. spider
                           9. arachnid

Please see the attached spelling homework sheet for the week. Have a terrific week.

Sincerely,

Mary P. Roberts

OPEN HOUSE NEWSLETTER

Usually, schools will hold an Open House within the first month of school. It is always helpful to have a packet of information ready for the parents to take home on this occasion. Include in the packet any information provided by your school district pertaining to objectives and goals for your grade level. Explain in your Open House letter the promotion standards for your grade level. Parents need to know what will be expected at the end of the year to earn promotion to the next grade level. It is also helpful to provide parents with results of any beginning-of-the-year assessment you have conducted to measure reading levels, mathematical ability, and so on.

In your Open House letter, make sure to give information about any special programs used in your classroom or in your school. For example, if your school uses certain computer programs, explain these programs and what the students will be doing with them.

Along with your Open House letter, have a packet of student work samples ready for parents to review. Parents will then have the opportunity to go over work completed by their child and ask any questions pertaining to work requirements, grading policies, or work review guidelines.

Many of your parents may be unable to attend Open House. For those parents not attending, be sure to send the Open House letter (see the example prepared for a first-grade classroom) and packet of materials home with their child the next school day. You may also want to include a handwritten note letting the parents know that you missed seeing them and would be happy to go over the information at their convenience.

Welcome to Open House!

Dear Parents,

The purpose of Open House is to give you more information regarding your child's school day and the contents of the first-grade program. I hope the video shown tonight has given you a feel for the kinds of activities your child participates in during a typical school day. This letter should answer many of your questions regarding the first-grade program.

You will be receiving a copy of *Curriculum Objectives for First-Grade Students*, a blue brochure developed by the school district. This brochure lists the first-grade objectives for English, computer skills, mathematics, science, social studies, and health education. All objectives listed in

the brochure will be covered this year in our classroom.

At the first-grade level, all objectives are covered within thematic units. Thematic units have a curriculumwide focus on a topic. Learning activities throughout the students' day can be linked to the theme of study. For example, in our 2-week bear unit, using bears and bear activities, the students will be exposed to the following mathematical objectives:

- ☑ count using one-to-one correspondence
- ☑ identify ordinal position
- ☑ make reasonable estimates of "how many"
- ☑ use directional/positional words
- ☑ describe likenesses and differences
- ☑ describe objects and their attributes
- ☑ create patterns of objects
- ☑ find and correct errors in patterns
- ☑ use nonstandard units to measure length
- ☑ gather, organize, and display information as a group
- ☑ answer questions about charts and graphs
- ☑ explore combinations for numbers to 10

In our mathematics program, we strive to cover the objectives using creative, hands-on approaches that keep students

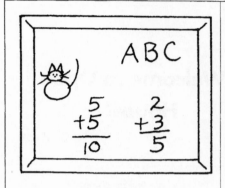

involved in an active manner. Activities are planned to move the students from the concrete to the symbolic level of understanding. Students will be tested so that they will be working on skills and activities that will challenge them and keep their interest.

At our school, we provide a *balanced literacy program*. We do this by providing students with opportunities each week to participate in shared, guided, and independent reading and writing activities. Students will also receive systematic instruction in phonics and spelling.

Each week your child will work in reading groups. These groups will consist of five or six children who use similar reading strategies and are able to read

similar levels of text without support. I will regularly assess your child's oral reading so that I will have your child reading the appropriate level of materials in these reading groups. The information gained in the assessment will dictate what skills need to be taught in the reading sessions.

At our school, we have a computerized reading comprehension program. This is a supplemental reading program. This reading program allows students to select books to read, either with a parent or independently, at home or during free reading time at school, and then take comprehension tests about these books using the computer. Books for this program can be found in the classroom and in the Media Center for student checkout. Once the student has read one of these books, he or she can take the comprehension test about the book using the computer. Students scoring 80% or greater on five or more tests each 9-week grading period will receive a free skating pass. Please keep in mind that this is a supplemental program. Students may sign up each morning if they desire to take a test. Tests will be administered when students have completed their regular classroom work.

In our classroom, students are encouraged to use transitional spelling in their creative work. Transitional spelling frees students to write without stopping for assistance. Students are encouraged to write the sounds they hear in words they want to use. The teacher then writes the message using *traditional spelling* underneath. By coming into contact with an increasing number of words in print throughout the year, students begin to replace the transitional spelling with traditional spelling on their own. In this packet, I have included an example of the growth in writing that can occur within a short period of time using this method. The two writing samples in this packet are works from one of my former first-grade students. Both pieces were completed independently by the student in response to listening to a literature selection. It is amazing what growth can occur in 5 months!

Social studies, science, and health will be integrated within the themes of study. Students will work with hands-on activities; with social studies, science and health texts; and children's literature to achieve objectives in these areas.

At the end of the first-grade year, your child will need to meet promotion standards to be considered ready for second grade. One of the promotion standards is that your child be able to read orally and comprehend a test book selected by our county. Your child will need to be able to read the test book orally with 90% or greater accuracy. He or she will also need to answer correctly five out of six comprehension questions related to the reading. I have set out examples of past test books and sample questions for you to view this evening.

Nightly reading is very important in first grade! Each night, part of your child's homework will be to read for 15 or 20 minutes. Select a time when you can devote your full attention to your child. These uninterrupted few minutes are very important. Take time to talk about the cover of the book before you start to read. Point out the name of the author and the illustrator. If your child has not previously read the story, ask him or her to predict what the story will be about on the basis of the cover illustration. Discuss those predictions as you complete the reading.

The reading of the story can be done in a number of ways, depending upon the purpose of the reading and your child's current reading skills. Next week, I will be sending home a packet of information that will assist you in helping your beginning reader, developing reader, or independent reader continue to grow with the reading process.

Thank you for coming to Open House this evening. Few things are more important than your participation in your child's education! It is also important to keep the lines of communication open between home and school. Please, do not hesitate to contact me, either by note or by calling me at school (555-5835) if you have questions regarding your child. We share the common goal of wanting your child to have the best first-grade experience available!

Sincerely,

Mary P. Roberts

September 19, 1995

I liked it wen the Little Girle Had her frist ben.

"I liked it when the little girl had her first dream."

(Student art)

Wednesday, February 28, 1996

Mount Rushmore is in
South Dakota. The
people who made it
got dynamite and
stuck it in the
rock to get peices
of the rock off.
First someone was
going to make
hero's on the
mountian but some
one had a better
idea. It was to
put presidents on
the mountian. The
presidents were o
Goerge Washington,
Thomas Jefferson,
Abraham Lincoln and
Teddy Roosevelt.
It took more
than ten years
to carve Mount
Rushmore. Mount
Rushmore is a
symbol,

Very
Good!

NOTE: I rewrote the entire selection using traditional spelling, grammar, and punctuation
for the child on the opposite page of this journal entry.

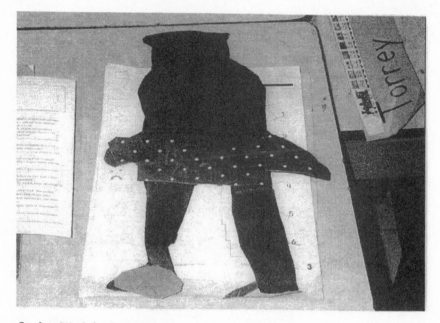

Student Work for Open House

OPEN HOUSE VIDEO

Parents always want to know what a "typical day" in the classroom is like. It is so much easier and more meaningful in this instance to show rather than tell. In the week or weeks prior to Open House, videotape a variety of activities in your classroom. Make sure to get all students on film while you are working on this project. You can show students working independently, participating in lessons, singing songs, sharing their work with other students, and playing on the playground. Once you have a wide variety of things taped, you can view and edit the video to get it ready for presentation.

Prior to making this video, talk to your principal about any written permissions you may need in order to photograph or videotape the children in your classroom. Your principal may have a standard form that could be used or could help you develop one.

When editing, look at the footage through the parents' eyes. Select the things that you know will appeal to them. Always include some type of introduction and conclusion to your video. You can work on this when the children are not present. For example, you may tape the front of your school building as you give your introduction. While you are taping, you can narrate the introduction by inviting the parents inside to see what happens in your school and classroom on a typical day.

You might have the students make an attractive sign with the slogan "Thank you for coming to Open House" to tape for your conclusion. The students can hold up the sign and chant the saying.

Make sure to keep in mind how much time you will have to show the video. If you will have parents in your room for 30 minutes, you will want no more than 20 minutes of video. This will give you and the parents time to interact before and after viewing the video. The parents will thoroughly enjoy the video.

CONFERENCES

There will be many occasions throughout the school year when you will need to meet with parents for conferences. Some conferences will be at your request. Other conferences will be at the parents' request.

If having conferences with all parents of your students is not a requirement of your school district, you will find it very helpful to meet with a member of each of your students' households at the end of the first grading period. You can schedule these conferences before school, after school, or during workdays.

To begin, make a schedule of days and times you will be available for conferences. Send a note home to each family requesting the best times for them to meet with you. Using the family's input, assign each family one of your available times. Send home a form with each child indicating the purpose of the conference, the date, and the time. Have a portion of the form as a tear-off piece that the parent can sign indicating intentions to attend the conference or a request for another conference date and time. A sample is provided on the next page.

Once you have scheduled the conferences, you will need to prepare for them. Being well prepared lets you make effective use of the conference time. Prior to conferences, it is often helpful to send home a questionnaire to the parents. Let them know that the information gathered will help in preparation for conferences. Ask parents such questions as what their child likes best about school, what he or she likes least, what any special concerns are that the child has expressed at home about school, what concerns the parents might have, and so on. Design your questions so that there will be equal representation of positive and negative responses. By using the questionnaire, you will know your parents' concerns ahead of time and will have the necessary time to gather materials to share with parents about their concerns. This also allows you simply to have the time to think about your responses and not be caught off guard. For example, if a parent expresses concerns about the district's use of transitional rather than traditional spelling, you would have the time to get a copy of the district policy and rationale as well as any research you might have supporting the use of transitional spelling in the primary classroom.

It is often helpful, to both you and the parents, if you prepare a conference report for each conference prior to the conference date. The conference report is a

First Quarter Conference Schedule

Dear Parents,

To better serve both you and your child, I will be holding parent-teacher conferences over the next 3 weeks to go over your child's progress in the classroom and to answer any questions you have regarding the first quarter of the school year.

In order to meet with each of you, I have come up with a conference schedule and assigned each family a conference date and time. If you will be unable to attend the scheduled conference, please let me know so we can attempt to reschedule the conference to better meet your needs.

Your conference has been scheduled for _____ at _____:_____ a.m./p.m. In Room _____. I greatly look forward to meeting with you.

- -

Please return this portion to school with your child.

Student's Name _____

I will attend the conference scheduled for _____ at _____:_____ a.m./p.m.

I will be unable to attend the scheduled conference. Please contact me to arrange a different conference date and time. You can best reach me by:

_____

Parent's Signature: _____

tool to help you remember points you want to focus on during the conference. You may wish to fill in your conference reports while doing report cards or while reviewing student work and anecdotal records. Examples are given on the following pages of a conference report for a high-achieving student and a report for a low-achieving student.

Place the conference report in front of you during the conference. This way, you may glance to the conference report as a reference to make sure you cover all of the information you wish to cover during the conference. It also is helpful to make a copy of the conference report, prior to the conference, for the parent to take home.

After going over the contents of the conference report, address any items from the questionnaire that you feel need to be covered. Share any pertinent information that you have collected in response to the parents' concerns. This will show parents that you are responsive to their concerns and needs.

Following your discussion of the conference report and questionnaire, ask parents if they have questions about the information you have shared with them or about something that you have not covered. Make sure to answer all questions firmly and confidently. Always present yourself in a professional manner when answering parents' questions. If you are genuinely unsure of an answer, let the parent know that you do not have that information at this time, but you will find the answer to the question and let him or her know as soon as possible. At that point, make a note to yourself. This will let the parent know that you have heard his or her question and will pursue the matter. Always be sure to follow up on the question as soon as possible to give the parent the information he or she was seeking.

There will be occasions when a conference is at the parent's request and not yours. It is helpful if you do not go into the conference blindly. When a parent asks you for a conference date and time, simply ask the parent what the subject of the conference will be. Let the parent know that it will be helpful for you to know the subject in advance so that you will be able to gather materials to prepare for the conference. Usually, parents will be more than happy to let you know prior to the conference what they wish to discuss. It is always better not to be taken off guard. If you know 2 days prior to the conference that you will be discussing a controversial subject, you will have time to confer with administration and possibly to request that an administrator sit in on your conference.

Conferences will be your best way to gather and share information with parents throughout the school year. You will learn more about your students' home life during a 15-minute personal conference than you could learn all year through the student, written communications with the parents, or telephone conferencing. Make good use of this valuable communication tool.

There will be many reasons for you to have conferences with students' parents. You will meet with parents to share academic as well as behavioral concerns. You

Conference Report

Date of Conference: *October 21*

Conference held with: *Janet Simmons*
Conference was called at the teacher's request.

Regarding (Student's Name): *Matthew Simmons*

Things that are going well:
Matthew is doing an excellent job with addition and subtraction facts with sums to 18. Matthew is reading and comprehending work on or above grade level. Matthew's written work has shown growth since the beginning of the school year. Matthew loves working with experiments in science.

Things we are working on:
We are working on having Matthew use proper punctuation and capitalization in his written work. We would also like to see more use of detail and elaboration in Matthew's written work. In mathematics, we will continue to work with above-grade-level materials with Matthew in order to meet his needs.

Things to do at home:
Have Matthew check his homework assignments for proper use of punctuation and capitalization. Encourage elaboration in Matthew's written work. Continue having Matthew select chapter books for nightly reading.

Parent's Signature:_____

Conference Report

Date of Conference: *October 22*

Conference held with: *John Smithers*

Regarding (Student's Name):   *Johnny Smithers*

Things that are going well:
Johnny is very enthusiastic about school and learning. Johnny performs well in cooperative groups. He demonstrates strengths in leadership skills in the classroom. This is most evident during science exploration activities. Johnny is working on grade level in mathematics. He eagerly participates in mathematics lessons and especially enjoys the hands-on activities.

Things we are working on:
Johnny is currently reading below-grade-level materials. We are working on Johnny's current instructional reading level to develop a greater variety of reading strategies. Johnny is working with the phonetic strategies (sounding out unknown words), yet he is not currently using any other strategies (such as rereading for meaning and using picture clues and clues in text).

Things to do at home:
Have Johnny tell you what is happening on each page of the book by using the pictures prior to actually attempting to read the page. Encourage Johnny to go back to reread a sentence when he comes to a word he is having difficulty sounding out. Have Johnny make guesses as to what word(s) would make sense in the sentence. Have Johnny try several strategies to figure out unknown words before you supply him with the correct response.

Parent's Signature: _____

will meet with parents of children with special needs. You will meet with parents with reasonable as well as unreasonable requests. For whatever reason, all of your conferences will go more smoothly if you are well prepared and maintain confidence and a professional attitude. Always keep in mind that you are a professional.

TELEPHONE COMMUNICATIONS

You will have three occasions on which to call parents on the telephone. You will need to call parents to return their phone calls, to convey positive information, and to convey negative information. When you call parents of your students, make sure you are in a situation where you have plenty of uninterrupted time to discuss the matter. Call from school after the children have left, or call from home when you have no distractions. Avoid calling parents at their workplaces unless it is an emergency or the parent has asked you to use the work number.

Make sure to return parental phone calls as soon as possible. If the parent is agitated about something, delaying the return call will only feed the agitation. If the phone call does not seem to be solving the problem, invite the parent in for a conference to discuss the matter further.

Make sure to make positive phone calls. Parents are often shocked, sometimes to the point of being nearly speechless, to receive a call from school regarding great things their child has done. Every child in your classroom should receive at least one positive phone call during the school year. You may wish to call to report that a child's spelling grade has shown significant improvement. You may also call a parent to tell of tremendous growth in a child's positive behavior. After completing any positive phone call you will feel great, the parent will feel great, and after the phone call, the child will feel great!

Unfortunately, many times when you contact a parent on the telephone, you will be conveying negative news. Always make sure to call a parent regarding consistently poor behavior. Many times the parent will immediately take care of the situation. If possible, it is very effective to call a parent from school when you have the child present. Inform the parent that you have his or her child with you, the child has been misbehaving, and you thought the parent could speak with the child on the telephone to let the child know of the parent's expectations for school behavior. More times than not, this will cure the problem instantaneously.

Whether you return a phone call, call with positive news, or call with negative news, always document phone calls in a documentation log. Your documentation log can be a notebook set aside to list all communications with parents. After making a phone call, in the notebook simply write the date, the parent's name, and a brief summary of the conversation. You may need to refer back to this documentation if there ever is a discrepancy or if the student is tested for further educational services.

Let parents know the best way to contact you. Give parents the best times you can be reached at school. Thirty minutes before school, after school, and during your planning periods might be some of the best times for you to receive phone calls at school. If you have e-mail capabilities at school, you may wish to give your e-mail address to parents as an alternative for contacting you.

WRITTEN COMMUNICATIONS

In order to avoid playing phone tag with parents, it will be helpful to let them know that the best way to get in touch with you is by sending a note to school with their child. In this way, the parent will be sure that you receive the message as soon as possible. Check with your students at the beginning of each day for notes. Make sure that you, in turn, respond to any notes that day by either returning a written message or making a phone call if that seems necessary.

When sending written messages that you need the parent to sign and return to school, always make a copy of the message before sending it with the child. Designate a basket or other container to store all signed notes and copies of notes sent to parents. Then, if there is ever any question regarding the message sent home, you will have an easily accessible copy of the note.

BRIDGING THE COMMUNICATION GAP

There will be families that you will work with who will be more difficult to communicate with than others. Many families in the United States are non-English-speaking or limited-English-speaking families. Some of your students' parents may also have difficulty reading and writing. You will need to find ways to overcome the obstacles in communicating with these parents.

One of your first steps for bridging the gap is to find out what resources your school and school district offer for communicating with families who are non- or limited-English-speaking. You may find a wealth of support. Many school districts provide teacher training in this area. You may find that there are interpreters either at your school or in your school district who can assist you. There are computer programs available that can translate standard teaching forms into many different languages.

Sometimes a neighbor or older sibling in the family who speaks the same language, as well as dialect, can interpret the information you send home for the parent or serve as an interpreter during a conference. This method of using a neighbor or older sibling can also work for families in which parents have difficulty reading and writing. You will need to make sure to handle these matters with care. Many parents who have limited literacy skills are embarrassed about this. Find a tactful way to approach the matter.

If your school has a phone message machine for calling parents to convey information, you can create messages for parents needing this service. You may also call interested parents personally to give weekly or monthly updates.

The most important thing to keep in mind is that you and the families you work with need a way to communicate effectively with each other. It will be up to you to find the resources to make this possible. Such effective two-way communication is a must for children's success in your classroom. Through thoroughly and professionally communicating aspects of the educational program, you will gain the respect of parents, colleagues, and school administrators. The time and effort you put into parent communications will be invaluable.

3

Parent Involvement

Many parents of children, especially in the primary and early educational years, want to be involved in their child's education as much as possible. This desire goes beyond just wanting to help their child complete homework assignments. Your communication with the parents of your students, as highlighted in the previous chapter, will help. Many parents will want to be even further involved.

Keep in mind that many children in today's society do not live in two-parent homes. Some children live with grandparents, other relatives, foster parents, or others. Find out the living situations of your students. If children cannot have a member of their immediate family involved in the school program, they may have another adult of great importance to them who would be able to be involved.

Parents and loved ones of your students unable to come to school to be involved may wish to be involved and help in other ways. These parents could help by cutting out materials, preparing booklets for student use, or preparing other classroom materials.

Several easy ways to get parents and other loved ones involved in their child's classroom and education are: recruiting parents as tutors of students needing additional support, asking parents to take part in the curriculum by being speakers or readers, asking parents to join the class at lunch, and asking parents to serve as chaperons on field trips.

PARENTS AS TUTORS

A positive way to get parents involved in your classroom is to ask interested parents to serve as tutors for students needing extra support. Tutors should be available to work with a student on a regular, consistent basis throughout the school year.

To recruit classroom tutors, you may wish to send a letter home asking for volunteers. You might also wish to discuss this need at parent-teacher meetings. Once you have recruited tutors, you will need to let your classroom tutors know how you would like them to help their students.

It would be helpful if you could plan a training session for all volunteers. This session will enable you to assign each volunteer to a student, assign a location for the tutoring sessions, and go over any information regarding what you would like the tutors to accomplish during tutoring sessions. The training session would be a good time to stress the importance of the confidentiality needed for the protection of the students being worked with.

If your school and school district allow this, it is usually best if the tutoring sessions take place outside of the regular classroom. By choosing a different location, the tutor and students are not distracted by what is going on in the classroom, and the regular classroom activities are not disrupted by the presence of the tutor. Prior to your meeting with volunteers, see your school administrator to find out what areas might be available for tutoring sessions. If the tutoring sessions must take place within the classroom, find an area of the room that will minimize distractions for the student being tutored as well as for the rest of the class.

Once the tutors have met with you to go over preliminary information, you will need to be prepared for each visit of a classroom tutor. Often, teachers will lose valuable instructional time each week when a tutor enters the classroom. The teacher often breaks away from the students to confer with the tutor about what they would like to be done that week with the student. This is a problem that can easily be avoided.

Make a box for each student who will be regularly tutored. Place supplies such as writing paper, pencils, crayons, scissors, and glue in each box. Also, place some reading material that can be used by the tutor after completing the planned activities.

Each week, plan either review or enrichment activities for the tutors to use. These activities should support what you are doing in the classroom. Write easy-to-follow, specific directions for your tutors. Place the directions, along with additional needed supplies, in each child's box.

Leave a notebook in each child's box. Tutors should be encouraged to use the notebook for writing a short note to you at the conclusion of each tutoring session. This will enable the tutor to communicate with you regarding the tutoring session without pulling you away from the other students.

Tutoring boxes should be placed near the entrance to your classroom. In this way, the tutors may enter the classroom each week, quietly call the student they will be working with, and have all the necessary directions and materials, causing minimal disruption. Tutors can return materials to the classroom in the same manner.

PARENTS AS GUEST SPEAKERS OR READERS

One easy way to get parents involved is to invite them to speak on a subject they are knowledgeable about. Many parents enjoy discussing their jobs, careers, or hobbies. At the beginning of the year, you could send home a questionnaire asking parents what their area of expertise is that they would be willing to share with your class. Then, at a time of the year when this subject could be tied into what you are working on in the classroom, you could invite the parent to be a guest speaker.

Another easy way to get parents involved is to invite them to share their children's favorite books with the class. This would be a great activity to do after lunch. A parent could come and read to your students for 15 to 20 minutes. The parents could read either selections brought from home or something you provide. Students thoroughly enjoy having guest readers.

Prior to a visit from a guest speaker or reader, talk with the parent about exactly what will be discussed. This will help you to avoid any unnecessary surprises and to screen for age appropriateness of materials.

PARENTS AS LUNCH BUDDIES

Parents of young children often enjoy joining their child for lunch in the school cafeteria. Let your parents know the days and times when they can come to eat with their child. You may have students whose parents are unable to join them for lunch during the school day. It is nice if you allow visiting parents to have lunch with their child plus one other child who does not have a parent who is able to come to school. Everyone involved in this activity will have a great experience.

PARENTS AS CHAPERONES AND CLASSROOM HELPERS

You will often have occasions when you will need "extra hands." This may be in the classroom during special activities or when leaving the school campus for field trips. Let parents know well ahead of time that you will need assistance. Parents could let you know by phone call or in writing that they are interested in helping with the special activity or field trip. More information regarding using parents as special helpers will be given in Chapter 11, "Planning for Special Events."

DEALING WITH CONFLICTS

Unfortunately, when dealing with parents, even the best teachers can experience conflicts from time to time. If you get into a situation where there is a conflict with a parent, always keep your cool. You must maintain your professionalism. If a conflict arises, do your best to calm the parent. If the parent does not seem to be cooling down, it might be helpful to schedule a conference for a later date to discuss the matter further. By scheduling for a later date you will be able to confer with colleagues and administrators for guidance regarding the matter prior to speaking again with the parent. The time delay will also give the parent time to cool off. Don't stay alone in the classroom with an irate parent. Let the parent know that you will need either to go and get an administrator involved to continue or to reschedule for another time. Always inform your administrative team when conflicts arise. Your administrators will be able to give you guidance and may need to intervene to help solve the problem.

You will find that most parents and other loved ones will enjoy being involved in classroom activities. Parents like to feel welcomed in their child's school. Many like to feel like they are making a contribution. You will find that using parents as tutors, as guest speakers and readers, as lunch buddies, and as chaperons will be easy ways to get the parents involved while assisting you with what you want to accomplish.

4

Discipline

Discipline is always a main concern for both newly hired and seasoned teachers. Maintaining a well-managed classroom environment is an absolute necessity to promote learning. Students do not thrive in a classroom filled with discipline problems. Once discipline problems arise, students are not learning as much as they should be learning.

There are several requirements to providing a well-disciplined classroom. You will need to have a clear set of rules and consequences, provide structure throughout each day, and have tools to use for students who have difficulty following rules even in the best of circumstances.

RULES AND CONSEQUENCES

Rules for the classroom can either be schoolwide rules, rules you have predetermined necessary for your students, or rules you work with the students to generate. Students should understand that rules are necessary in order to help everyone in the classroom learn and exist in a healthy environment. Your main classroom rules should be short, easily understood by your students, and directed at most foreseeable problems.

For example, your classroom rules might be:

1. Raise your hand.

2. Keep hands, feet, and objects to yourself.

3. Walk, do not run.

4. Use good manners.

5. Respect others.

Classroom rules should be posted in the classroom at all times. Make an attractive, easy-to-read chart listing classroom rules. Everyone entering the classroom will be aware of the expectations for behavior in your classroom.

Once you have designated your classroom rules, you will need to have a management system that provides positive feedback as well as letting students know when they have broken the rules. This management system needs to be easily accessible to you during teaching and highly visible to the students.

Large posterboard charts are a feasible suggestion. You will need to make two charts for your class. One chart will be used to show rule infractions. The second chart will be used to show positive behavior points. To make classroom management charts, simply adhere a library pocket for each student in the classroom to posterboard. Write a student's name on each library pocket.

For the rule infraction chart, you can use a traffic light system. Make tags to fit in each child's library pocket out of green, yellow, and red durable cards. These should be laminated. As with a traffic light, green means go, yellow is a warning, and red means stop. Each morning, students in your classroom will begin with a green tag. It is important for students to start each day fresh. Students will want to keep this green tag all day to demonstrate their fine behavior. If students break rules, you will change the color of their tags in the following manner.

> 1 yellow tag in pocket = warning
> 1 red tag in pocket = loss of 5 minutes of recess time
> 2 red tags in pocket = loss of all recess time
> 3 red tags in pocket = parent is contacted
> 4 red tags in pocket = office referral

Make sure to post the meanings of the tags in the classroom. You will also need to convey this information to parents so they will know what it means when their children come home and say that they kept their green tags all day. This information can be sent several times during the year in the weekly newsletter.

The second chart will be used to catch students doing the right thing. Place 3 x 5 index cards in each library pocket. As you go through the day, point out children who are using good line manners, working quietly within groups, sharing nicely with a friend, and so on. Whenever you catch someone doing the right thing, thank

SOURCE: Cutouts by Punkydoodles, Hewitt, Texas. Reprinted with permission.

them for helping the community of learners, and use a hole puncher to punch a hole in that child's index card. A hole can also be earned by a student each day that student keeps his or her green tag all day. To reward good behavior, all students earning at least five hole punches per week will get to participate in a fun activity planned for Friday. The fun activity could be a snack, extra center time, a visit to the classroom treasure box, or playing games brought from home. Students will work to gain the number of hole punches needed to participate in these activities. Students not earning the required number of hole punches do not participate. Another reward that can be given based upon hole punches is a Student of the Week award. The student or students earning the greatest number of hole punches in a week can be awarded a Student of the Week certificate. When presenting the Student of the Week certificate, give the recipient public thanks for making the classroom a better place to learn.[1]

STRUCTURE

Providing an organized, structured, well-planned, and engaging learning environment for your students will cut potential discipline problems by an estimated 90% or more. If the students know that you hold high expectations for their behavior, if they are engaged in meaningful and fun learning activities, and if they have minimal opportunities for off-task behavior, you will have won the majority of the battles.

Each day, prior to the students' arrival, you will need to be completely prepared for that day's activities. This means all activities will need to be planned, all materials for each lesson should be ready and easily accessible, and alternative activities need to be ready for students finishing work early. One strategy would be to have a box or bin with all materials needed for the day placed in it in order of need. Many times students have problems controlling their behavior if classroom transitions from activity to activity are not handled smoothly. To keep students engaged, activities planned for the day need to vary between passive listening activities and more active activities.

No matter how well you have planned or how experienced you are, there will always be one or two challenging students in your classroom. Many students entering school for the first time have not had any prior experiences with following rules and meeting expectations. Also, family expectations for behavior may be different from your expectations. Some students' energy levels make it difficult for them to comply with the school's expectation that they sit for long periods of time.

Knowing your students and their backgrounds is essential in helping students meet your expectations in the classroom. It is important to find the cause of inappropriate behaviors. Talk to the child's parents about what you have observed and see if you can work together to try to find possible causes of behaviors. Then, working together, you can form a plan of action.

Perhaps a child having severe temper tantrums is acting in this manner due to sleep deprivation. Many children stay up too late to have a productive day in the classroom. You would need to approach the parents to discuss your observations and ask for their assistance in identifying possible causes and forming interventions such as getting the child to bed at an earlier hour.

Changes in this child's behavior will not be noted until the need for sleep is met. Sometimes, even after contacting a parent, this type of problem will continue. You might need to address the issue at school by letting the child nap at school at a convenient time. Always make sure your administration is aware of situations like this. Ask for guidance and ideas to remedy the problem. Children cannot learn if their basic needs for sleep, food, and safety are not being met. Make sure to be sensitive to these issues.

DOCUMENTATION

If the tag chart system coupled with parental communications is unsuccessful in maintaining a student's behavior, you will find it an absolute necessity to document steps you have taken or are taking to correct the student's behavior. A school administrator will be much more likely to take a hard stance if you have good documentation than if you send a student to the office without any information regarding the steps you have already taken to help the student follow classroom rules.

To document student behaviors, prepare a notebook to record interventions you have used in the classroom with the student. Since this is confidential information, keep this notebook in a secured location.

For example:

Johnny Smith

10/20

Johnny lost his recess today due to calling out in class, disturbing tablemates, and rough play on the playground. He had two red tags on the tag chart, which resulted in his loss of recess.

10/22

Johnny, after having two red tags on his tag chart, threw a crayon at a tablemate. After school today, I had a phone conference with his mother. I let her know of the behaviors that I witnessed and discussed a plan to send a note home with Johnny each day to be signed by her.

10/23

Johnny was sent to time out in another teacher's classroom for 15 minutes today for refusing to follow the directions of the teacher. After the 15-minute time out period, Johnny reentered the classroom and did a fine job.

10/24

Johnny hit another student on the playground this morning. The other student's injury required first aid. Johnny will be referred to the office, in accordance with policy, for this offense.

With this documentation, you may be able to see patterns that will help you determine causes of misbehavior. The documentation might show a chain of misbehaviors. You will also show administrator's efforts, on your part, prior to an office referral, to correct the unwanted behaviors. You may include this information in your office referral report, or you may simply wish to make a copy of your documentation notes to attach to the office referral report.

Another form of discipline documentation that can have a positive effect on student behavior is the daily checklist. Students experiencing difficulties with specific behaviors may benefit by having a daily checklist. A daily checklist focuses on specific areas the student is having difficulty with. It enables the child to focus on improving those specific areas while giving the child's parent daily feedback on the child's progress in specified areas.

For example, if you have a student who has had difficulties with hitting other children, pushing in line, and talking back to the teacher, the daily report might look like this:

Daily Report for: _____ Date: _____	
Today I . . .	
kept my hands to myself on the playground.	_____ yes _____ no
walked in line in my own personal space.	_____ yes _____ no
talked to teachers respectfully.	_____ yes _____ no
Teacher's Comments:	
Parent's Comments:	
Parent's Signature: _____	

If one of your students is having difficulties managing his or her time to complete necessary school assignments, his or her checklist might look like the one below:

Daily Report for: _____ Date: _____	
Today I . . .	
entered the classroom quietly.	_____ yes _____ no
got ready for morning instruction.	_____ yes _____ no
completed my journal work on time.	_____ yes _____ no
completed assigned reading group work.	_____ yes _____ no
used my time wisely during independent working time.	_____ yes _____ no
Teacher's Comments:	
Parent's Comments:	
Parent's Signature: _____	

When filling out a student's daily checklist, you can either check the appropriate responses or use stickers for areas in which the child did a good job. Small star-shaped stickers, found in most schools and office supply stores, work well for this purpose. Write comments to give extra feedback about areas where the child had marked a "no" response. You can write a comment so the parent knows the particular circumstances that resulted in the "no" rating for that day.

Prior to sending home a daily checklist with the student for the first time, you will need either to meet with the parent or to discuss in detail over the telephone the reasoning behind the daily checklist. Let the parent know that the child is not functioning well behaviorally in your classroom. Explain that the daily checklist will be a tool to help the child focus on correcting his or her behavior in targeted areas, to communicate daily with the parent regarding the child's progress, and to document the child's behaviors should administration need to be called upon.

Using these guidelines will help you provide a structured, orderly environment for your students. This type of atmosphere is a must for promoting learning. Start by establishing your rules, consequences, and management system. Convey this information thoroughly to students and parents. Provide the structure and planning necessary to run an orderly classroom. When problems arise, always make sure to document your interventions. Intervention and documentation need to begin as soon as you see that a child is having repeated problems with following the classroom rules. Also, look for ways that you may need to change what you are doing. If a student frequently acts out during reading instruction, it may be his eyes, lack of skills, or misunderstanding of the directions you are giving. Students deserve the very best climate in which to work and learn. Do all you can do to provide it.

Note
1. This plan was adapted from *Assertive Discipline: Positive Behavior for Today's Classroom*, 1992, by Lee Canter and Marlene Canter.

5

Instructional Planning

Planning for instruction will be one of your major duties as an educator. Your school district will provide guidelines and a framework for what should be taught over the course of a year for your grade level. Even with this guide, much of the instructional planning will be up to you.

You will need to begin your planning by mapping out an overview of the year. List each month and week of the school year and begin to plug in themes and objective areas that you plan to cover in that frame of time. You may wish to involve your students in this process by asking them what themes they would like to cover during the school year. This plan does not need to be set in stone. As you begin working with your students, you will need to modify the plan to take into account the pacing of your students.

After working out your long-range plan, you will work to plan specific units or periods of time. This will be the time to set up a lesson plan book detailing each lesson that will be taught in your classroom. Schools often supply lesson plan books, but they can also be purchased at teaching supply stores. Even if your school supplies lesson plan books, you may find a format you prefer in some of the other lesson plan books offered on the market.

LONG-RANGE PLANNING

When planning the year, if teaching thematically, you will need to decide which themes you would like to cover with your students. You should make a plan at the very beginning of the year that shows the themes you will use. Under the umbrella of themes, you can plug in the skills that your county/district requires. A sample map of themes to be used in a primary grade classroom for an entire year is shown. Major skills to be covered are also included.

Theme: Back to School   **One-week unit**   **August**

Literature Selection   Author

This Is the Way We Go to School   Edith Baer
Arthur Goes to School   Marc Brown
Arthur's Teacher Trouble   Marc Brown
The Principal From the Black Lagoon   Mike Thaler
The Teacher From the Black Lagoon   Mike Thaler
Timothy Goes to School   Rosemary Wells

Major Skills and Activities

Literacy: Creative writing
                      Initial consonants

Mathematics: Graphing
                      Counting

Science/Health: Identifying safety rules

Social Studies: Social skills: rule setting and expectations
                      Making democratic decisions

Visual Arts: Making self-portraits

Theme: Back From the Beach: A School Picnic   **One-week unit**   **August**

Literature Selection	Author
The Teddy Bear's Picnic	Jimmy Kennedy
The Picnic	Mercer Mayer
Peanut Butter and Jelly: A Play Picnic	Nordine Bernard Wescott (Illustrator)
Blues #1 Picnic	Buster Yablonsky

Major Skills and Activities

Literacy:	Creative writing Initial consonants Rhyming Words
Mathematics:	Using number words to ten Numeral identification
Science:	Sorting and classifying
Social Studies:	Social skill: planning a picnic
Visual Arts:	Designing invitations

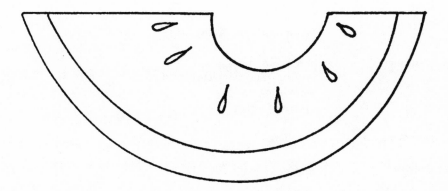

Theme: Kevin Henkes Author Study   One-week unit   September

Literature Selection   Author

Chrysanthemum   Kevin Henkes
Sheila Rae the Brave   Kevin Henkes
Chester's Way   Kevin Henkes
Owen   Kevin Henkes
Weekend at Wendel's   Kevin Henkes

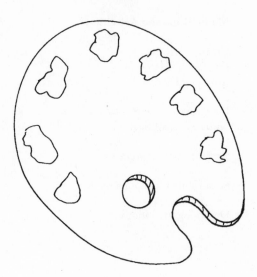

Major Skills and Activities

Literacy: Initial consonants
                       Writing using complete sentences
                       Sequencing events
                       Creative writing

Mathematics: Graphing

Science: Creating and reading information from charts

Social Studies: Predicting consequences of actions

Visual Arts: Painting using watercolors

Theme: Bears   **Two-week unit**   **September**

Literature Selection   Author

Koalas   Caroline Arnold
Pandas   Norman Barrett
Little Polar Bear   Hans de Beer
Numbears   Kathleen Hague
Old Bear   Jane Hissey
The Teddy Bear's Picnic   Jimmy Kennedy
Brown Bear, Brown Bear   Bill Martin, Jr.
The Best-Loved Bear   Diana Noonan
Bears   Kate Petty

SOURCE: Uchida of America, Corp. Reprinted with permission.

Major Skills and Activities

Literacy: Identifying works of fiction and nonfiction
                   Sequencing events
                   Creative writing

Mathematics: Patterning
                   Estimating/checking
                   Counting
                   Addition using manipulatives
                   Sequencing numbers

Science: Recalling factual information
                   Identifying animal survival requirements

Social Studies: Map skills

Visual Arts: Making bear pictures using geometric shapes

Theme: Magnets   **One-week unit**   **September**

Literature Selection   Author

Beginning Fun With Magnets   Gayle Bittinger
What Makes a Magnet?   Franklyn Man Branley
Science With Magnets   Helen Edom
What Magnets Can Do   Allan Fowler
Magnets   Steve Parker

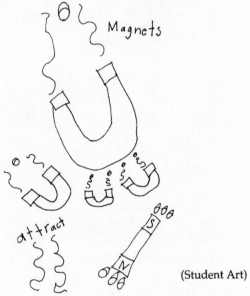

(Student Art)

Major Skills and Activities

Literacy: Informational writing
                   Initial consonants

Mathematics: Measuring using nonstandard units
                   Addition and subtraction with sums to 10

Science: Free exploration with magnets
                   Sorting magnetic and nonmagnetic materials
                   Recalling factual information
                   Making predictions

Social Studies: Social skill: working in cooperative groups

Visual Arts: Making informational posters

Theme: Lois Elhert/Fall Author study   **Two-week unit**   **September**

Literature Selections   Author

Feathers for Lunch   Lois Elhert
Fish Eyes   Lois Elhert
Nuts to You   Lois Elhert
Red Leaf, Yellow Leaf   Lois Elhert
Fresh Fall Leaves   Betsy Franco
The Reasons for the Seasons   Gail Gibbons
Why Do Leaves Change Color?   Betsy Maestro

Major Skills and Activities

Literacy: Creative writing
                     Creating a fall counting book
                     Final consonants

Mathematics: Addition and subtraction with sums to 10

Science: Identifying signs of each season
                     Describing what causes the seasons

Social Studies: Completing an assignment using division of labor

Visual Arts: Creating leaf prints

(Student Art)

Theme: Apples/Fall	One-week unit	October

Literature Selection		Author
The Seasons of Arnold's Apple Tree		Gail Gibbons
What's So Terrible About Swallowing an Apple Seed?		Harriet Lerner and Susan Goldhor
The Giving Tree		Shell Silverstein
Apple Picking Time		Michele B. Slawson

Major Skills and Activities

Literacy:	Sequencing events
	Comprehension
	Writing events in proper sequence
	Short a vowel sound

Mathematics:	Patterning

Science:	Graphing (real, picture, and bar graphs)
	Making predictions
	Forming and testing hypotheses

Social Studies:	Identifying wants and needs

Visual Arts:	Creating collages

Theme: Creepy Crawly	Two-week unit	October

Literature Selection	Author
The Very Hungry Caterpillar	Eric Carle
There's an Ant in Anthony	Bernard Most
Amazing Spiders	Alexandra Parsons
Backyard Insects	Millicent E. Selsam and Ronald Goor
Two Bad Ants	Chris Van Allsburg

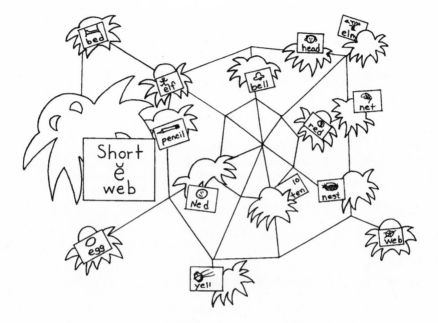

Major Skills and Activities

Literacy: Comparing and contrasting
                     Initial and final consonants
                     Short a and **e** vowel sounds

Mathematics: Adding and subtracting with sums to 10

Science: Recalling factual information
                     Describing life cycles

Social Studies: Comparing and contrasting social groups

Visual Arts: Creating three-dimensional insects and arachnids

Theme: Pumpkins   **One-week unit**   **October**

Literature Selection   Author

Jack-O-Lantern   Miriam Frost
It's Pumpkin Time   Zoe Hall
The Biggest Pumpkin Ever   Steven Kroll
Big Pumpkin   Erica Silverman
Pumpkin, Pumpkin   Jeanne Titherington

Major Skills and Activities

Literacy: **Short e** vowel sound
                   Sequencing
                   Identifying characters
                   Comprehension
                   Creative writing

Mathematics: Estimating/checking
                   Place value

Science: Describing life cycles

Social Studies: Identifying goods and services
                   Field trip to a pumpkin farm

Visual Arts: Making paper bag jack-o-lanterns

Theme: I Spy   **Two-week unit**   **November**

Literature Selection   Author

I Spy   Jean Marzollo
I Spy Christmas   Jean Marzollo
I Spy Fun House   Jean Marzollo
I Spy Gold Challenger   Jean Marzollo
I Spy Mystery   Jean Marzollo
I Spy School Days   Jean Marzollo

Major Skills and Activities

Literacy: Creating riddles
             Rhyming words
             Reviewing **short a** and **e** vowel sounds

Mathematics: Identifying two- and three-dimensional shapes

Science: Identifying properties of objects
            Sorting materials according to properties
            Classifying

Social Studies: Describing scarcity of items

Visual Arts: Creating an "I Spy" set

Theme: Thanksgiving/Nutrition   **Two-week unit**   **November**

Literature Selection   Author

Arthur's Thanksgiving   Marc Brown
A Turkey for Thanksgiving   Eve Bunting
The Legend of the Indian Paintbrush   Tomie dePaola
What's on My Plate?   Ruth Belov Gross
The Pilgrim's First Thanksgiving   Ann McGovern

Major Skills and Activities

Literacy: Short vowels: **a, e, i, o, u**
             Comprehension
             Identifying fiction and nonfiction

Mathematics: Patterning

Science: Following the digestive process

Social Studies: Social skill: table manners

Health: Labeling the food pyramid
           Creating a balanced meal

Visual Arts: Using Indian symbols

Theme: Penguins   Two-week unit   December

Literature Selection   Author

Mr. Popper's Penguins   Richard and Florence Atwater
A Wish for Wings That Work   Berkeley Breathed
Penguins   Gail Gibbons
Tacky the Penguin   Helen Lester
Penguin Pete   Marcus Pfister
Little Penguin's Tale   Audrey Wood

Major Skills and Activities

Literacy: Writing a friendly letter
                           Sequencing events
                           Comprehension
                           Creative writing

Mathematics: Fact families
                           Graphing

Science: Recalling factual information
                           Reading information from charts and graphs

Social Studies: Map and globe skills

Visual Arts: Making craft penguins

**Theme:
Jan Brett/Winter Author Study   Two-week unit   December/January**

Literature Selection   Author

Annie and the Wild Animals   Jan Brett
Christmas Trolls   Jan Brett
The First Dog   Jan Brett
Fritz and the Beautiful Horses   Jan Brett
The Mitten   Jan Brett
The Wild Christmas Reindeer   Jan Brett

(Student art)

Major Skills and Activities

Literacy:

Sequencing
Writing book reports
Identifying story elements

Mathematics:

Addition and subtraction of double-digit numbers

Science:

Identifying wild and tame animals

Social Studies:

Predicting consequences of actions

Visual Arts:

Creating an illustration with borders

Theme: Treasure Seekers   **Two-week unit**   **January**

Literature Selection   Author

The Treasure Hunter   William Boniface
Pirate Soup   Erica Farber
Tough Boris   Mem Fox
Grandma and the Pirates   Phoebe Gilman
Edward and the Pirates   David McPhail
Sheep on a Ship   Nancy Shaw

Major Skills and Activities

Literacy: **Long e** vowel sound
          Recalling factual information
          Sorting works of fiction and nonfiction
          Identifying characters
          Identifying settings
          Identifying problems
          Identifying solutions

Mathematics: Place value
          Identifying and giving values to coins

Science: Cataloging treasure

Social Studies: Using maps to answer questions

Visual Arts: Constructing pirate ships

Theme: Weather   **Two-week unit**   **January/February**

Literature Selection   Author

Cloudy With a Chance of Meatballs   Judi Barrett
Fortunately   Remy Charlip
Feel the Wind   Arthur Dorros
Weather Words   Gail Gibbons
Focus on Weather and Climate   Barbara Taylor
What's the Weather Like Today?   Rozanne L. Williams

Major Skills and Activities

Literacy:	Identifying story elements
	Identifying exaggerations in tall tales
Mathematics:	Copying simple designs
	Using a thermometer
Science:	Identifying different types of weather
	Naming causes of weather
	Using weather information in newspapers
	Predicting weather
	Checking predictions
	Forming and testing hypotheses
	Conducting experiments
Social Studies:	Map skills
Visual Arts:	Creating weather symbols using pattern blocks

Theme: Colors   **One-week unit**   **February**

Literature Selection   Author

Color	Ruth Heller
Little Blue and Little Yellow	Leo Lionni
M&M Counting Book	Barbara B. McGrath
Jelly Beans for Sal	Bruce McMillan
The Big Orange Splot	Daniel M. Pinkwater
My Many Colored Days	Dr. Suess

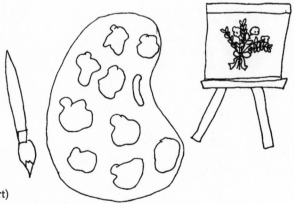

(Student art)

Major Skills and Activities

Literacy:

Creative writing
Long u vowel sound

Mathematics:

Estimating
Counting sets of coins

Science:

Mixing primary colors
Graphing
Interpreting graphed information

Social Studies:

Looking at neighborhood relationships

Visual Arts:

Making maps of neighborhoods

Theme: Valentine's Day   **One-week unit**   **February**

Literature Selection	Author
Arthur's Valentine	Marc Brown
The Valentine Bears	Eve Bunting
Arthur's Great Big Valentine	Lillian Hoban
Will You Be My Valentine?	Steven Kroll
My Funny Book of Valentines	Margo Lundell
One Zillion Valentines	Frank Modell
Valentine Mice	Bethany Roberts
Valentine Friends	Ann Schweninger
What Is Valentine's Day?	Harriet Ziefert

Major Skills and Activities

Literacy:

Contractions
Sequencing events
Comprehension
Quotation marks

Mathematics:

Sorting
Graphing

Science/Health:

The function of the heart

Social Studies:

Investigating holidays

Visual Arts:

Creating pop-up Valentine's Day cards

Theme: Dental Health   **One-week unit**   **February**

Literature Selection	Author
Tooth Fairy Magic	Joanne Barkan
Little Rabbit's Loose Tooth	Lucy Bate
The Berenstain Bears Visit the Dentist	Stan and Jan Berenstain
Arthur's Tooth	Marc Brown
Going to the Dentist	Anne Civardi and Stephen Cartwright
The Missing Tooth	Joanna Cole
Loose Tooth	Steven Kroll
How Many Teeth	Paul Showers

Major Skills and Activities

Literacy:	Short and long vowel sounds Predicting events Creative writing
Mathematics:	Adding and subtracting with sums to 18
Science/Health:	Dental health awareness Recalling factual information Choosing healthy snacks
Social Studies:	Careers (Dentistry)
Visual Arts:	Making papier-mâché teeth

Theme: Verna Aardema/African Folk Tales, Author Study   **Two-week unit**   **March**

Literature Selection	Author
Bringing the Rain to Kapiti Plain	Verna Aardema
Princess, Gorilla, and a New Kind of Water	Verna Aardema
Why Mosquitoes Buzz in People's Ears	Verna Aardema
Postcards From Kenya	Helen Arnold
A Story, a Story	Gail E. Haley
A Is for Africa	Ifeoma Onyefulu
Abiyoyo	Pete Seeger

(Student art)

Major Skills and Activities

Literacy:	Rhyming words
	Identifying story elements
	Completing vowel sorts
	Making inferences
Mathematics:	Copying simple designs
Science:	Studying animal habitats
Social Studies:	Map and globe skills
Visual Arts:	Making African animals using clay

Theme: Fairy Tales **Two-week unit** **March**

Literature Selection Author or Retold by

The Frog Prince Rose Impey
Jack and the Beanstalk Rose Impey
Hansel and Gretel James Marshall
Red Riding Hood James Marshall
The Three Little Pigs James Marshall
The Frog Prince Continued Jon Scieszka
The True Story of the Three Little Pigs Jon Scieszka
Cinderella William Wegman
Lon Po Po Ed Young

Major Skills and Activities

Literacy: Comparing and contrasting
Completing vowel sort
Identifying elements of fairy tales
Creative writing
Comprehension
Sequencing events

Mathematics: Place value
Adding and subtracting double-digit numbers

Science: Labeling the life cycle of the frog

Social Studies: Social skill: cooperation

Visual Arts: Creating a poster for a favorite fairy tale

Theme: Eric Carle Author Study **Two-week unit** **April**

Literature Selection Author

The Foolish Tortoise Richard Buckley
The Greedy Python Richard Buckley
The Grouchy Ladybug Eric Carle
A House for Hermit Crab Eric Carle
The Mixed-Up Chameleon Eric Carle
My Apron Eric Carle
The Tiny Seed Eric Carle
The Very Hungry Caterpillar Eric Carle
The Very Quiet Cricket Eric Carle

Major Skills and Activities

Literacy: Compound words
                    Creative writing
                    Sequencing events

Mathematics: Telling time to the hour and the half-hour
                    Graphing

Science: Recalling factual information
                    Measuring
                    Creating and reading charts
                    Observing life cycles of living things

Social Studies: Predicting consequences for actions

Visual Arts: Creating collages using pages made with watercolor

---

Theme: Dinosaurs   **Two-week unit**   **April**

Literature Selection   Author

Literature Selection	Author
Count-A-Saurus	Nancy Blumenthal
Dinosaurs	Gail Gibbons
I Can Read About Dinosaurs	John Howard
Bone Poems	Jeff Moss
If the Dinosaurs Came Back	Bernard Most
Whatever Happened to the Dinosaurs?	Bernard Most
A Boy Wants a Dinosaur	Hiawyn Oram and Satoshi Kitamura
The Dinosaur ABC Book	Jerry Pallotta
Dinosaur Babies	Lucille Recht Penner
Mrs. Toggle and the Dinosaur	Robin Pulver
The Meat-Eaters Arrive	Suzan Reid
Ten Little Dinosaurs	Pattie Schnetzler
Tyrone the Horrible	Hans Wilhelm

Major Skills and Activities

Literacy:

Comprehension
Creative writing
Vowel digraphs

Mathematics:

Adding double-digit numbers

Science:

Using charts to locate specific information
Measuring
Graphing
Interpreting graphed information
Researching

Social Studies:

Making democratic decisions
Using map skills to show where dinosaur bones
have been discovered

Visual Arts:

Making papier-mâché dinosaurs

Theme: Ruth Heller/Living Things
Author Study   Two-week unit   **May**

Literature Selection   Author

Literature Selection	Author
Animals Born Alive and Well	Ruth Heller
Chickens Aren't the Only Ones	Ruth Heller
How to Hide a Crocodile	Ruth Heller
How to Hide a Parakeet	Ruth Heller
Kites Sail High	Ruth Heller
Many Luscious Lollipops	Ruth Heller
Merry-Go-Round	Ruth Heller
Plants That Never Bloom	Ruth Heller
The Reason for a Flower	Ruth Heller

Major Skills and Activities

Literacy:	Identifying nouns
	Identifying verbs
	Identifying adjectives
Mathematics:	Identifying open and closed figures
Science:	Identifying living and nonliving things
	Discussing animal camouflage
	Identifying mammals
	Identifying egg-laying animals
	Discussing needs of living things
Social Studies:	Identifying goods and services
Visual Arts:	Using art media to camouflage an animal

Theme: Environments   **Three-week unit**   **May/June**

Literature Selection	Author
Where the Forest Meets the Sea	Jeannie Baker
Life in the Deserts	Lucy Baker
Life in the Oceans	Lucy Baker
Life in the Polar Lands	Lucy Baker
Life in the Rainforests	Lucy Baker
This Is Our Earth	Laura Lee Benson
The Magic School Bus Hops Home	Joanna Cole
Antarctica	Helen Cowcher
Rain Forest Secrets	Arthur Dorros
Recycle!	Gail Gibbons
Geography From A to Z	Jack Knowlton
Earth Songs	Myra Cohn Livingston
Ming Lo Moves the Mountain	Arnold Lobel
The Desert Alphabet Book	Jerry Pallotta
The Sun, the Wind and the Rain	Lisa Westberg Peters
The Lorax	Dr. Seuss
Forest Animals	Luise Woelflein

Major Skills and Activities

Literacy:	Comprehension Vowel digraphs
Mathematics:	Measuring Graphing
Science:	Identifying characteristics of environments Describing food chains Discussing the importance of recycling Identifying recyclable items Selecting correct animal habitats
Social Studies:	Map and globe skills Identifying geographical features
Visual Arts:	Designing posters of favorite environments

This mapping out of books to be used, activities to be done, and skills to be covered by no means encompasses everything that will be done in this primary grade classroom in a year. This is merely a skeletal framework ready for the construction of the entire academic program. The teacher can use this outline to get a sense of pacing, a structure, and some idea of the materials needed for specific areas. Once this is done, more specific short-range planning can begin.

SHORT-RANGE PLANNING

Short-range planning consists of the plans made 1 or 2 weeks in advance for each instructional day. It is important to be well planned for at least a week or two ahead of time. However, it is difficult to plan farther in advance than this because you need to take into account the level of mastery your students demonstrate with the material presented. You may need to change your plans to allow more time for specific skills, or less time, depending upon the needs of your students.

Make it a habit to plan 2 weeks ahead of time. This may seem difficult at first, but it is a great habit to start right away. By planning 2 weeks ahead of time, you will be sure to have your copies run off well before you need them, have time to gather materials for upcoming units, and make necessary booklets and supporting materials for your activities. School copying machines are notorious for breaking down. If you have planned well ahead of time, you will not find yourself in a bind if this or other unforeseen circumstances occur.

Short-range lesson plans can be completed in a lesson plan book. Your school may have specific requirements pertaining to how you complete lesson plans. Make sure you check into your school's guidelines prior to making lesson plans.

Most lesson plan books are already formatted to set up organized lesson plans easily by the days of the week. They are further divided so you can list specific subjects for each day. See the examples of completed lesson plans for a first-grade classroom on the following pages.

TEAMWORK IN PLANNING

Teaching is better as a team effort. Teaching should be about not competition but collaboration. Many of your best creative endeavors will not be entirely your own. Always refer to a variety of teaching resources for ideas. Some of your best resources will be located in your school. These resources are your colleagues. All teachers bring their own individual styles and experiences to their planning. Working closely with your colleagues will enable you to gain and share ideas for presenting information to students in more effective and creative ways. You will grow as a professional by working with your team. Working with other teachers on your team will also enable you to share in the workload of planning instructional activities.

When working with other teachers on your grade level, it is helpful to work together to form a system that will ensure that all participating teachers contribute to the planning session and come to each planning session prepared. It is very frustrating for a team member to spend time prior to a team planning session getting materials ready and developing activities to share, only to find that not all members of the team have come prepared to plan. This leads to wasted time and resentments. An agreement by all team members on what is expected, prior to the meeting, will be a necessity.

It may be helpful for you and your team to develop a planning form and guidelines to meet your specific planning needs. For example, four first-grade teachers decided they needed to come up with a planning form that would cover the things they wanted to plan together. They wanted to plan together activities for reading groups, math, whole group literature, and centers and developed the first-grade planning form shown on the next page.

Prior to each planning session, the general theme or subject needs to be decided upon so all teachers will be planning activities for the same theme. By completing the planning form prior to the planning session, all teachers have done their "homework" and are prepared to share ideas on the theme. Also, by making

Table 5.1 Sample Lesson Plans

	Reading Groups	Spelling/Phonics Instruction	Language Experience/ Literature Activity
Monday	GROUP ONE: Students will read the first five chapters of *Storm!* Students will complete teacher-made activity independently.	Students will make words using the letters in *Weather Watchers*. Materials: individual letters for students, recording sheets	Play "What is in the box?" Place an umbrella in a box prior to lesson. Materials: box, umbrella, chart paper, pens, paper
Tuesday	GROUP TWO: Students will read the first five chapters of *Storm!* Students will complete teacher-made activity independently.	Students will generate lists of words containing the vowel digraph **ea.** Separate the list into **long e** and **short e** words.	Discuss weather terms the students are already familiar with. Read *Weather Words.* Complete rainbow forms. Materials: *Weather Words,* rainbow forms, chart paper
Wednesday	GROUP THREE: Students will read *Umbrellas.* Students will work with the teacher to answer questions using complete sentences.	Students will complete phonics worksheet p. 56 to identify words containing the **ea** vowel digraph.	Read the big book *What's the Weather Like Today?* Use an interactive chart to work with the days of the week. Students will write their own verses. Materials: big book, student sheets, interactive chart, days-of-the-week cards
Thursday	GROUP FOUR: Students will read *Why?* Students will read and illustrate each line of the story.	Students will write sentences using words containing the **ea** vowel digraph.	Read *Cloud Book.* Look at types of clouds (poster). Go outside to observe clouds. Photograph clouds. Compare photographs to poster. Identify cloud types. Use cotton and other media to make cloud types. Materials: *Cloud Book,* camera, film, poster, cotton, glue
Friday	GROUP FIVE: Students will read *Why?* Students will read and illustrate each line of the story.	Students will take a spelling test of **ea** words assigned this week.	Read *Feel the Wind.* Students will write four facts about the wind on a pinwheel pattern.

Table 5.1 Sample Lesson Plans (continued)

Math	Science	Notes
Students will make a class picture graph depicting their favorite type of weather. Materials: chart paper, index cards, crayons	Students will work with a demonstration thermometer to read temperatures. Complete math thermometer worksheet p. 71.	Learning Centers for the week: 1. Dictionary Search 2. Filmstrip (*Cloudy With A Chance of Meatballs*) 3. Science Exploration (Tornado Tube)
Students will use class graph made yesterday to answer specific questions.	Students will work in groups to form and test a hypothesis. Place one thermometer in the shade and one in the sun. Read pp. 14-15 of *Weather and Climate*. Form and test hypotheses.	4. Math Center (Dice Toss Game) 5. Math Center (Make patterns using weather stamps)
Students will use pictures of elements of weather to solve fact family facts. Materials: pictures of weather elements, fact family worksheets	Read *Weather Watch*. Pass out maps of North America. Label countries of North America. Students will use small weather stickers to show weather corresponding to the newspaper weather forecast map.	
Students will solve fact family facts without the aid of pictures. Materials: fact family worksheets	Read *Raindrops and Rainbows*. Make rain using a teakettle, burner, trays, ice, and food coloring. Students will write about what they observe.	
Students will use pattern blocks and pattern block pieces or stickers to create pictures about weather. Materials: pattern blocks, pattern block pieces, construction paper, glue	Read *Magic School Bus at the Waterworks*. Discuss the water cycle. Set up water cycle experiment using zip lock bags, water, and blue food coloring.	Friday Fun Activity: Make cloud dessert with whipped topping and chocolate pudding. Use a champagne glass for each child.

copies of your work for each participating teacher, each teacher will walk away from the planning session with all the necessary instructions and handouts needed for all the ideas brought to the meeting.

You do not have to use all of the ideas discussed at the planning session. Choose the activities that appeal to you. Also look for ideas that will best meet the needs of your students. Always save the planning forms and handouts for future

FIRST-GRADE PLANNING FORM

Theme:_____

Literature Activity:_____

Book Title: _____

Where book is available: _____

Activity: _____
_____
_____
_____

Math Activity: _____
_____
_____
_____

Centers: _____

First Center: _____

Objective: _____

Activity: _____
_____
_____

Second Center:_____

Objective: _____

Activity: _____
_____
_____

Guided Reading: _____

Book Title: _____

Number of copies available: _____

(Continued)

First Grade Planning Form (*continued*)

Location where books are available: _____

Activity: _____

_____

_____

_____

_____

_____

Please make a copy of this planning form for each team member as well as one copy of any handouts needed. Please bring these to grade-level planning session.

---

reference and use. Make a file for each theme and keep everything. You might not want to use something this year, but it might be more intriguing or better suit the needs of your students next school year.

PLANNING FOR A SUBSTITUTE

There will be occasions when you will be unable to be in the classroom due to personal illness, family emergency, or attendance at a workshop. It is important that you leave specific, easy-to-follow lesson plans for your substitute. Lesson plans, whenever possible, should reflect what you would be doing in the classroom if you were there. Well thought-out plans will provide the structure and continuity absolutely necessary for your students to have a meaningful, productive day in your absence.

Keep in mind that the substitute may be coming to your school for the first time. Make a "substitute folder" that includes such things as a copy of your daily schedule, a classroom roster, a seating chart, name tags for students, a map of the layout of your school, emergency procedures, a duty roster, and the name of a teacher or other helper to contact for further assistance.

The above information, your daily lesson plan, and all materials needed for the activities you have planned need to be placed in a specific location for the substitute. You may want to place all of the items in a plastic tub or a large notebook. If you plan to be out for several days, you may want to label paper grocery bags with each date and place that day's materials inside. An example of a daily lesson plan left for a substitute is shown on pages 75-77.

Substitute Lesson Plans for Wednesday

7:15-8:00	(Students will begin entering the classroom from the buses and cars at 7:15. Students will arrive in the classroom any time between 7:15 and 7:50.)
	Write the date on the marker board. Students should write an entry in their journals (kept in their desks). Students who finish early may either read silently at their desks or go to a computer station.
8:00-9:00	Call students to the carpeted area. Read and discuss the story *Alexander and the Wind-Up Mouse*. Write the following on the board:

Think of a time you were looking for something. Write a story to describe that time.

Read the writing prompt to the students, pointing to each word as you read. Let the students know that the purpose of this exercise is to practice writing to a prompt. (We are getting ready for our end-of-year writing assessment and I want to give the students practice with the writing test format and procedures.) Demonstrate folding a sheet of paper in half twice to create four panels. Draw pictures of the sequence of a time you were looking for something. Model writing a story about a time you were looking for something. Pass out paper folded into quarters and writing paper, located on the shelf near the window. Ask the students to share orally what they are going to write about. Have students complete the prewriting activity of sequencing events of their stories on the paneled paper. Allow students to take their time with their writing. Remind students to remember the capitalization and punctuation rules they have been learning. Also, remind the students to use their best handwriting. Students who finish their work early may illustrate their stories on the back of the writing paper. When a majority of the class have finished writing their stories, let students volunteer to come to the front of the room to share their stories orally with the class.

Note: Several students will be entering and exiting the room at odd times during this period (due to work with special teachers and/or tutors). You may choose to either engage them in the group activity or have them go to the computer or the listening center if they are entering at an inconvenient time.

9:00-10:30	Call the students to the carpeted area. Let the students know that they will be listening to a story and answering comprehension questions about the story. Prior to reading the story, read the questions that will need to be answered. Complete a shared reading and discussion of *Ming Lo Moves a Mountain*. Pass out mountain-shaped step books, comprehension questions, and sequencing paper. Read each question orally to the students. Demonstrate how to glue the question pieces onto the mountain step book. I have left an example for you. Students should glue the questions onto the mountain step book and then lift up flaps to answer the questions. Students should be encouraged to answer the questions using complete sentences. Students who finish early may illustrate their work.

Go over sentences and pictures on the sequencing worksheet. Students should color pictures, cut out strips, and glue them in proper sequence on construction paper.

10:30-11:00	Art Students need to be taken to the art room (Room 211) for art class. Have students take their lunch boxes/money to art class, as they will go directly from there to lunch. You will not need to stay with the students during this time. Pick up students promptly at 11:00.

11:00-11:40	Lunch (in cafeteria)

11:40-12:00	Quiet Time Ask students questions about the previous day's reading of *The Mouse and the Motorcycle*. Ask students to predict what they think will happen in today's chapter. Read the next chapter of *The Mouse and the Motorcycle* to the students. This book is located on the television stand. Discuss it.

12:00-12:55	Math Review Activity Pass out shapes and geometric solids BINGO sheets used yesterday. Have students swap their BINGO board with a friend. Pass out plastic beans to be used as markers. Call out the names of shapes and geometric solids to play BINGO. After playing in this way, have students call out spaces by giving clues (for example, I am a flat shape with three sides; A birthday hat is in my shape; etc.) The winner of each BINGO game may be sent to the treasure chest to collect a prize.

Pass out sheets of geometric solids and geometric solids graph.

Have students make a graph of geometric solids to check for understanding.

12:55-1:25   Recess
Take students to the primary playground and supervise them during play time.

1:25-1:55   Science
Pass out science books (located under science center table). Have students read pp. 22-24 with a partner. Discuss causes of erosion. Ask students what effects erosion would have on Ming Lo's mountain. Have students work with their partners to answer the questions on p. 24 in their science journals (located in students' desks).

1:55-2:00   Get ready for dismissal by making sure students have their homework folders, have checked out a book for nightly reading, and have gotten their book bags, lunch boxes, and coats.

Students may use the remainder of the time for show and tell.

2:00   Dismissal
Walk both bus students and car riders to the front of the building. Dismiss the bus students first. Stay with car riders until the buses have pulled out. Car riders then need to be escorted to the lower traffic circle. You may leave the car riders under the supervision of the teachers and staff on duty.

Note: The extra work on my desk is in case you run out of things to do. Don't worry if you don't get everything I have planned finished today. I just want to make sure you have enough to do. I would rather leave too much than too little. Please leave a note for me letting me know what assignments you completed. I hope everyone has a good day. Thank you.

A substitute will appreciate the time you put into writing such specific lesson plans. Your students will benefit by having things run as smoothly as possible in your absence. By completing easy-to-read, specific plans, a day with a substitute will not be a lost day or a day simply to be written off.

If you work on a computer, it may be helpful to save portions of a substitute lesson plan for future use. For example, if your students work in journals each day from 7:30 until 8:00, there is no reason to type this over each time you make a substitute lesson plan. You may wish to create a template. When creating a template, include all information that will not change from one day to the next. In this way, you will be able to access your saved template, and in doing so, save yourself some time.

Even if your school does not require you to have emergency lesson plans on hand in the event that you cannot get lesson plans to school for your absence, it is a very good idea to put the time into creating emergency lesson plans. Emergency lesson plans need to include a day's worth of activities and materials for your students. When creating emergency lesson plans, you will need to plan activities that could be completed at any time during the school year. For example, you would not want to include activities specifically dealing with autumn because your plans might not be used until spring. You may wish to include activities such as a writing assignment, a comprehension or sequencing activity, a math game or puzzle, a cooperative group activity, and so on. If your school does not have a central storage area for housing emergency lesson plans, leave them with a neighboring teacher. Make sure you have that teacher's home telephone number so you can call to let him or her know that your substitute will be needing your emergency lesson plans that day.

Creating emergency lesson plans may take time and effort at the hectic beginning of the year, but you will be especially thankful you took the time if you wake up one cold, November morning with the flu. Rather than dragging yourself out of bed, trying to figure out what your students will do that day, you will just need to make one quick phone call. Then, you can go back to bed.

PLANNING FOR THE FIRST DAY OF SCHOOL

The first day of school will be a mixture of excitement and even a bit of terror for both you and your students. Young children can be very intimidated by a new school setting. Your first day will be of the utmost importance in setting the tone for the year. You need to make sure, no matter what your feelings of insecurity may be, that you face the day with an air of confidence. Let your students and their parents believe that you know exactly what you are doing. You will best accomplish this by being very well prepared for the first day. Know exactly what you will be doing every minute of the day. Have every supply—every piece of construction paper, every pencil, every book, every glue bottle—ready ahead of time. There will be no time in the day to collect needed supplies. Plan more activities than you'll ever need for that day. It is always better to be overplanned than to be underplanned! Extra activities can always be saved for another day; however, running out of things to do can lead to chaos!

Parents who share your excitement and apprehension will escort many of your students on the first day. Some may have difficulty letting go and may wish to linger in your classroom. Often, this lingering creates more stress for the child than calm. If a parent of a distressed child shows concerns about leaving the classroom, assure the parent that the child will be in good hands and will do just fine after the parent leaves. If the parent still shows feelings of discomfort, invite the parent to leave for a period of time and then peek in once things have gotten under way.

The most hectic part of the first day of school will be when the students are arriving. It is important to have inviting, engaging activities set up for the students to participate in immediately upon arrival. These activities should be ones that students can engage in with minimal directions and supervision. You will be pulled in many different directions in the first half-hour of the first day.

You may wish to place different activities in different areas of the room. For example, one table could be covered with several puzzles that students could put together. Another table could be loaded with different art supplies such as decorative markers, plain paper, coloring pages, and colored pencils. A third table could be filled with wooden blocks for children to play with. A fourth area could have many attractive, child-friendly books for reading.

As children enter the classroom, let them know what the choices of activities are and have them choose a station to work in. Let the students know that they will continue to work in that one station until you ask them to move to another activity. This will cut down on the likelihood of children's jumping from activity to activity. It will minimize movement in the classroom and start the day in an organized manner.

Once all students have arrived, begin your first whole group activity. Students want to know about you as a person. Before the first day, make a poster about yourself. Include photographs of your family, your home, your pet, fun times that you have had, and your hobbies. You may wish to use magazine pictures for things you don't have photographs for. Write captions on the poster to go with the pictures. Your poster can be displayed in the classroom near the front entrance. Parents visiting your classroom will also be interested in the poster.

For your first whole group activity, have the students come to the common seating area. Take time to tell the students about yourself. Share the poster with the students. Allow students to ask any questions they might have. Let the students know that you would like them to make a poster about themselves this week for homework to bring into the class to share.

Give each student a page of story writing paper. Have them go to their desks to draw and/or write about one thing they would like to include on their poster. After the students have finished with their product, let them introduce themselves and tell about their pictures and stories. This activity will serve as a getting-acquainted activity as well as give you your first indication of their skill levels.

It is very important, early in the day, that you discuss your expectations for the students. Go over all classroom rules with the students. Rules may be either teacher- or class-generated. Whatever your rules are, make sure the students know that you have nothing but high expectations for their behavior. Let students know that rules are necessary for everyone in the classroom to feel safe and respected.

Try to find an appropriate children's book to use as an introduction to your focus on rules. Find a story in which a character has a hard time because he or she did not follow the rules. In your discussion of the story, let students lead the conversation to things that would be needed to have an orderly classroom and why this is necessary. Discuss why good behavior choices are important.

Once you have discussed the importance and necessity of rules, it will be time to go over consequences for inappropriate behaviors. Show students your system for rule infractions. If you are using a tag chart, show students exactly how the tag chart works. If you write names on the board to signify warnings, time-outs, and so on, give specific examples.

As soon as you have thoroughly described your system for positive and negative consequences, put the practice into use. You will never have another first day of school this year. You must be very firm at the beginning of the year. Be stricter than you intend to be. Once students have settled into your routines and behavioral expectations, this will no longer be necessary. However, you cannot ever start off soft and then become firmer. It simply does not work. You are not intended to be the students' friend. You are their teacher. Your students need to know that you mean what you say and that you will be consistent. You will be loved and respected by your students if you run a well-disciplined classroom. The time and effort spent the first days of school will set the behavioral tone for the remainder of the year.

You have handled the arrival of students, completed the "getting to know you" activity, and explained your system for classroom management. It may feel as if you have put in a full day's work, but it is very likely that only an hour and a half has passed.

An enticing art activity would be a great thing to do at this point. For example, you may have already written the students' names on tag board pieces. Allow the students to decorate their names using colorful tissue paper, beans, and the like. Provide a variety of media to let the students' creativity shine through. You may wish to put the completed art projects on your word wall for students to use while learning each other's names.

Going to the cafeteria for the first time with young children can be an adventure beyond your wildest dreams. Before the first day of school, be well aware of your school's procedures for lunch. Children, especially young children, will need to be prepared for what is going to happen. It is advisable to give your students a tour of the cafeteria prior to their first lunch time. Take the students to the cafeteria that first morning just as you would at lunchtime. Demonstrate to the children how they will go through the cafeteria line and where they will sit. Explain your expectations for cafeteria manners. Show the children how to line up after lunch to go back to the classroom. This tour of the cafeteria may take some time, but it will save you time in the long run. Prior to taking the tour, discuss with your cafeteria manager what you plan to do. When lunchtime comes, your children will already know what to do. You won't have to flounder over procedures while two of your children have spilled their milk on the floor.

By this time, everyone, including you, will need some down time. Take your class to the playground for some well-deserved free playtime. Keep in mind that your students have had 2½ months to play and enjoy unstructured time. Before students are released to play, go over any boundaries, specific playground rules, and signals and expectations for lining up when recess is over. Again, be aware of your school's policies and guidelines.

Following recess, students should go back to the classroom to wash their hands. If there is not a sink in the classroom, allow time for students to wash their hands in the designated area before lunchtime. Allow students to get lunch boxes and money needed for lunch. Remind students of key points from the morning's cafeteria tour.

After lunchtime, students need to come into the classroom in a quiet, orderly manner. It is often difficult to get students back on track after lunch. A quiet rest period is a great idea for all primary students. After entering the classroom, students put their heads down on their desks for 5 minutes of quiet "rest time." This time can be spent listening to classical music or listening to the teacher read a chapter out of a chapter book. Once rest time is over, students will be ready to participate in your afternoon learning activities.

Your students will do well with a hands-on math activity following lunchtime. Prior to giving students manipulatives, go over your expectations for working with hands-on materials. You may wish to plan a fun activity where students sort candy according to color, size, or shape. Students can then construct a graph showing this information. When students finish with the activity, they may eat their manipulatives! You may also wish to give a type of math assessment to determine which skills from the previous year have been mastered. This will aid in planning for future mathematics instruction.

Following math, allow students to work in centers. For the first day, your centers can be the activities students worked with upon entering the classroom. You may wish to add your listening center and computer stations as choices. Go over the expectations, procedures, and management system for working in centers.

You may wish to make a poster of all center options. For each choice, have a clothespin for each space available in that center. When children select a clothespin, they go to the corresponding center. When all clothespins for a specific center have been taken, that center is full.

Following center time, give students directions for how you want daily journals to be kept. Model what you expect to be done in journals by completing your own journal entry on a large piece of chart paper. Students at any level of reading and writing can participate in this activity. Some students may be writing sentences independently. Others may be at the point of just writing strings of letters. Encourage students to sound out words they do not know how to spell. Have students orally list some ideas of things they would like to write about. Allow students time to write in their journals. Students can write about whatever they choose in their journals. You may require certain elements in journals each day such as the date, a certain amount of writing, and an illustration. Let the students know that from now on, each day upon entering the classroom, they will write in their journals. Let them know that this will begin on the second day of school.

Allow plenty of time to get students ready to go home on this first day. Do not give out homework or nightly assignments in the first week of school. The students have enough changes to adapt to without adding this. Before dismissal, allow students to share what they liked about the first day of school. This will leave the students with positive feelings and ideas to share with their parents about the first day. This will also serve to reinforce the learning and major points you covered on the first day.

Prior to the first day of school, it will be very helpful to you if you call each of your children's parents to introduce yourself and verify how the children will be getting home on the first day of school as well as for the remainder of the school year. By making these calls, you will feel secure that you know how to send each child home on the first day. Once all the students have been safely delivered to their transportation home, you can breathe a sigh of relief. You have made it successfully through one of the most challenging days of the school year! Enjoy it and then get yourself ready for day two.

PLANNING FOR A TYPICAL SCHOOL DAY

Providing a structured environment for students is as important as providing a foundation for a building. Your structure will greatly determine the success of your academic program. Young students thrive in a structured environment. A classroom can be a very active, interesting, and child-centered place while being structured.

You will need to provide a consistent, daily schedule that your students can become accustomed to and comfortable with. Students will know what to expect each day. Children gain a sense of security in this type of atmosphere. Below is an example of a daily schedule for a primary classroom.

8:00-8:30   Students arrive for the day. Students write and/or draw in their **journals.** Students may write about either a topic of their own choice or an assigned topic posted on the board. Journal time provides a quiet, consistent way to begin each school day. Beginning the day in a quiet manner sets the tone for the whole day.

8:30-9:00   Students participate in a **shared reading** assignment. The teacher reads a selected piece of literature. Students respond by completing a specific, related assignment.

9:00-9:45   Students go to **special classes** (P.E., Media, Music, Art).

9:45-10:00   Teacher presents **phonics** or **literacy** instruction. Students are assigned independent activities that will be completed during reading group time.

10:00-11:30	Students work on independent work. The teacher works with **reading groups** while the rest of the class works on independent activities or in centers.
11:30-12:00	**Lunch**
12:00-12:10	Students enter the classroom from the cafeteria. Students put their heads down on their desks for rest time. The teacher reads a chapter from a novel. This allows the students time to settle down from lunch time and to prepare for the remainder of the day.
12:10-1:15	Students participate in **mathematics** activities and lessons.
1:15-1:45	**Recess**
1:45-2:20	Students participate in **social studies, science,** or **health** lessons.
2:20-2:30	Students pack to go home. Teacher reviews homework assignments. Calendar activities are completed.
2:30-2:40	Students are **dismissed.**

Each day, the basic structure will remain the same. You can be flexible within your structure. It will not take long for your students to become familiar with the classroom routine.

PLANNING FOR THE END OF THE YEAR

It is just as crucial to have well-planned activities for the end of the school year as for the first day. It will be more important than ever to maintain structure for your students. Students have some difficulty with following rules and procedures at the end of the year. Excitement about the upcoming summer, changes in the weather and temperature, and special events planned for the end of the year all work primary students into somewhat of an end-of-year frenzy. This is no time for you to go easy on discipline or classroom routine!

Make sure to keep your daily routines the same until the very last minute of the school year. If you have done three reading groups each day since the beginning of the school year, make sure to continue doing these reading groups until the last day of the school year. Whenever possible, stick to your daily routine.

Save an interesting, hands-on theme for the end of the year. Make sure to plan to go over material and work on activities that both you and your students will be

SOURCE: Prang is a registered trademark of "Dixon Ticonderoga Company." Used with permission.

excited about. If you are not excited about the unit or subject, you will not be able to convey enthusiasm to your students. Depending on the weather in your area, you may wish to plan many outdoor learning activities for your students in the last weeks of school.

In the classroom, students will enjoy working on an end-of-the-year book. You can create your own end-of-the-year books. In their end-of-the-year books, students can have classmates sign autographs and give interviews. Students can write about their favorite subjects and things about that school year. If you have a class picture, or individual pictures of the students, this is always a nice thing to include in the end-of-the-year book. You can be creative and decide what you would like to include and have students complete for this project. Bind books in such a way that students will take them home as keepsakes.

Another fun activity for students to complete at the end of the year is to create a filmstrip highlighting the students' favorite activities or themes covered throughout the school year. Receipt tape, divided into sections, could be used for making the filmstrip. The filmstrip could then be threaded through a shoe box or other type of box for viewing.

It is also helpful if you can engage students in a special project for the last month of the school year. Perhaps you might plan to put on a play using information from one of your last themes of the year. By scheduling a performance for the last week of school, you will be able to have your students work together toward a common goal in the last month of school. Getting ready for a play generates enthusiasm in even the most reluctant student. Your students will be so busy creating scripts, creating set designs, and learning their parts, that they will have little time to engage in end-of-the-year "itis."

A bonus of presenting a play at the end of the year is that it gives closure for the parents. The play enables the parents to get involved in the performance and attend the performance with family members. It also gives them the opportunity to communicate with you about the school year if you have a visitation time following the performance.

Inviting the parents to school, whether you choose to put on a theatrical presentation or not, is a fantastic way to end the school year. You might have the parents come to lunch on a designated day or to a picnic. A book picnic is a winner with parents. To create a book picnic, simply take picnic lunches and books to the playground. When everyone has finished eating their picnic lunches, students will read their favorite books to their parents, family members, and friends. Those students who do not have family members or other loved ones attending can read to a friend's parents. This activity takes very little planning and preparation, yet is greatly enjoyed by all. If you decide to do a picnic, make sure to set a rain date in the event that the weather does not cooperate with you on the designated day.

The end of the school year should be an exciting time to reflect upon the current school year and make and share plans for the future. Make sure you do all that you can do with your planning and supervision of activities to guarantee that you, your students, and your students'parents are able to enjoy the end of the school year.

6

Developing Themes

Finding and creating the most interesting materials and methods for presenting information to students can be one of the most challenging and rewarding aspects of teaching. Students will be excited and interested in what they are doing only if their teacher is also. Students need to know that what they are learning is valuable and makes sense in the context of a "bigger picture." Teaching the subject areas through the use of themes is an ideal way to get students motivated to learn skills in specific areas.

To begin, look at the district curriculum for your grade level. Look for major concepts that can be used as themes to integrate all of the curricular areas. Once you have decided on appropriate themes, you can begin collecting materials.

Developing themes can be both time-consuming and expensive. If you are planning to make a career of teaching, it may serve you best to begin to purchase your own materials for themes. By purchasing your own materials, rather than relying solely on the public library or your school library, you will be able to depend on having the same books and materials to use from year to year. Activities that you invest time in creating can then be recreated each year if you have the proper materials.

Begin your collection slowly. There are many ways to begin to acquire children's literature and materials that will keep you within a budget. Your school may provide money for you to spend for classroom educational materials. Always check into this possibility first. You can begin a personal collection of children's books and related materials by participating in book clubs, scouring yard sales, and asking for books as gifts from the parents of the students you teach.

Most schools will receive information from book clubs for students. It is definitely worth your time as a teacher to participate in getting your children to order from these clubs. Many of these clubs provide teachers with free book picks just for ordering. Some clubs also award points toward paying for books for your classroom based upon the number of dollars spent by the students. Investigate the choices you have available at your school. If the school receives solicitations from more than one book club, find the one that will best meet your needs and those of your students. Look for the benefits to the teacher. Also, look to see which book club offers the best quality of children's literature.

Yard sales can be a teacher's dream. Often you will be able to find books, games, and puzzles at yard sales that can be used in your classroom. When looking for yard sales, select "young" neighborhoods where many children live. Remember when shopping yard sales that no price is firm. Always try to talk the seller down on the price.

Parents often give teachers gifts at holiday time and at the end of the year. If a parent ever approaches you to ask what you would like as a gift, ask for children's books related to topics you are interested in developing themes for. Some parents might even approach you at some point of the school year to ask what you might like donated to the classroom. Have in mind instructional materials you want in case this opportunity arises.

To get started without becoming overwhelmed, work on building your collection of books and materials for one or two themes a year. For example, after reviewing district guidelines and curriculum, you decide that you want to develop units pertaining to weather and dinosaurs. Everywhere you go, be on the lookout for books, games, puzzles, and activities dealing with weather and dinosaurs. With this focus, you will be able to build a nice collection for both themes at minimal cost. If you space your purchasing over a longer period of time, you will have the opportunity to comparison shop.

Once you have gathered materials from your personal collection, the public library, and your school library, you will need to make plans to use the materials to cover specific learning objectives for your grade level. Using a copy of your school district's course of study, determine which of these objectives can be taught using the materials under the theme of choice.

The following are activities planned for a primary grade classroom for a unit on weather. All activities support the required curriculum for this particular primary-grade teacher's students.

WEATHER UNIT

UNIT TITLE:	Weather
GRADE LEVEL:	First or second grade (may be adapted for third grade)

BROAD OBJECTIVES: The student will develop an appreciation of weather.
The student will become familiar with weather
terminology.

EVALUATION OF UNIT: Teacher observation and student participation
Accumulative assessment of daily activities

This is a thematic unit covering the areas of listening/speaking, reading, writing, social studies, science, math, art, and music.

Nonfiction Books for Weather Unit

Cosgrove, Brian, *Weather*. New York: Alfred A. Knopf, 1991.
Dineen, Jacqueline, *Natural Disasters: Hurricanes and Typhoons*. New York: Shooting Star Press, 1993.
Dorros, Arthur, *Feel the Wind*. New York: HarperCollins, 1989.
Kierein, Tom, *Weather*. Colombia, South America: National Geographic Society, 1994.
Martin, Claire, *I Can Be a Weather Forecaster*. Chicago: Children's Press, 1987.
Rowe, Julian, and Perham, Molly, *Weather Watch*. Chicago: Children's Press, 1994.
Sabin, Louis, *Weather*. Mahwah, NJ: Troll Associates, 1985.
Simon, Seymour, *Storms*. New York: William Morrow, 1989.
Taylor, Barbara, *Focus on Weather and Climate*. New York: Shooting Star Press, 1993.
Taylor, Barbara, *Weather and Climate*. New York: Kingfisher Books, 1992.
Vianna, Fernando, Ed., *The American Heritage First Dictionary*. Boston: Houghton Mifflin, 1980.
Wandelmaier, Roy, *Now I Know Clouds*. Mahwah, NJ: Troll Associates, 1985.
Wyler, Rose, *Raindrops and Rainbows*. Englewood Cliffs, NJ: Julian Messner, 1989.

Fiction and Poetry Books for Weather Unit

Aardema, Verna, *Bringing the Rain to Kapiti Plain*. New York: Dial Books for Young Readers, 1981.
Barrett, Judi, *Cloudy With a Chance of Meatballs*. New York: Aladdin Books, 1978.
Charlip, Remy, *Fortunately*. New York: Aladdin Books, 1964.
Cole, Joanna, *The Magic Schoolbus at the Waterworks*. New York: Scholastic Inc., 1986.
Frost, Robert, *Stopping by Woods on a Snowy Evening*. New York: Dutton Children's Books, 1923.
Keats, Ezra Jack, *The Snowy Day*. New York: Puffin Books, 1962.
Spier, Peter, *Peter Spier's Rain*. New York: Doubleday, 1982.
Tresselt, Alvin, *White Snow Bright Snow*. New York: Mulberry Books, 1988.
Williams, Rozanne L., *How's the Weather?* Cypress, CA: Creative Teaching Press, 1994.
Zolotow, Charlotte, *The Storm Book*. Mexico: Harper Trophy, 1952.

SUBJECT: INTRODUCTION TO WEATHER UNIT

OBJECTIVE: The students will ask effective questions and make
inferences based upon given information.

MATERIALS: 1 large cardboard box
chart paper

markers
1 umbrella
index cards
pencils
display of weather books, posters, games, puzzles, etc.

PROCEDURE: Prior to the lesson, the teacher will place an umbrella inside a large, cardboard box. The teacher will display a large, sealed, cardboard box. The teacher will direct the students to try to guess what is inside the box. The teacher will tell the students that they may ask questions to try to determine what is inside the box. All questions must be ones that can be answered with only **yes** or **no.** The teacher will give examples of appropriate questions for the activity. The teacher will give the students time to write three or more questions they want to ask on an index card. Once students have had time to think of three or more questions, the teacher will have volunteers ask questions pertaining to what is inside the box. Once the questioning has begun, students will be encouraged to add questions to their lists. The teacher will write the students' questions on the blackboard or on a large sheet of chart paper. Following each question, the teacher will write the **yes** or **no** answer. This questioning and answering will continue until the students have figured out what is inside the box. The teacher may need to give some clues and steer the students in the right direction along the way. Once students have figured out what is in the box, the teacher will tell the students about the new theme of weather. The teacher will show exciting materials for the theme and talk about some of the activities that the students will participate in while working with the new theme.

ASSESSMENT   Student questions on index cards
TOOLS: Teacher observation of appropriateness of questions

SUBJECT: SCIENCE

PURPOSE: The students will learn the following weather terms: wind, rain, thunder, lightning, rainbow, snow, hurricane, tornado, cloud, and fog.

BEHAVIORAL   1. The students will listen to an introductory book about weather.
OBJECTIVES: 2. The students will listen to a book describing frequently used weather terms.
                  3. The students will define different weather terms.
                  4. The students will write a weather definition using their own words.

5. The students will use a weather word in their own sentences.
6. The students will sort weather terms into *wet* and *not wet* categories.
7. The students will predict what weather terms will be present that afternoon.
8. The students will decide which predictions were best.

MATERIALS: 5 copies of Gail Gibbon's *Weather Words*
1 copy of Barbara Taylor's *Weather and Climate*
student recording sheets (rainbow form)
5 sets of word cards with the following words printed on them:

wind	rain	thunder	lightning
rainbow	snow	hurricane	tornado
cloud	sun	hail	fog

1 set of weather word cards and weather definition cards for each student

PROCEDURE: The teacher will read *Weather and Climate* to the students to introduce weather in general. The teacher will discuss weather throughout the reading. The teacher will model giving the definitions of certain weather words. The teacher will then read *Weather Words,* having students focus on the terms and looking for the one term they are most interested in.

Weather Words

Definition:_____

In my own words:_____

My sentence:_____

My word is_____ (*wet* or *not wet*).

My weather prediction is...

_____

The teacher will select a weather term. He or she will model writing the definition from the book, restating the definition in his or her own words. He or she will also use the weather term in a sentence. The teacher will have the students orally complete this process with several weather words to check for understanding. The teacher will place a copy of *Weather Words* on each table. The teacher will direct the students to complete the first three sections of their recording sheets by writing the given definition of the weather term on the first line, rewriting the definition in the student's own words on the second line, and writing a sentence with the weather word on the third line. The teacher will then circulate while students work to check for understanding and aid those needing assistance. When students have completed this task, volunteers should read what they have written to the class.

The teacher will tell the students that some weather words describe *wet* things and some describe things that are *not wet*. The teacher will give each table a set of word cards. The teacher will direct the students to sort the weather words into the categories *wet* and *not wet*. The teacher will monitor group work. He or she will ask each group if they can think of other words to add to the list and which category the words would belong to.

The students will be asked to make predictions for the afternoon's weather based upon what they see now and their knowledge of the weather terms presented in this lesson. Students will complete their recording sheets by identifying their weather word as *wet* or *not wet* on line four and listing their prediction for the afternoon's weather using the remainder of the recording sheet.

The students will be given a set of word cards and cards with proper definitions listed on them. The students will be directed to match the weather words with the correct definitions.

ASSESSMENT   Teacher observation of matching activity
TOOLS: Student recording sheets

SUBJECT: LANGUAGE/MUSIC

PURPOSE: The students will learn to use the terms: cloudy, rainy, windy, snowy, sunny, and foggy.
The students will review the names for the days of the week.

BEHAVIORAL   1. The students will participate in a shared reading of *What's the*
OBJECTIVES: *Weather Like Today?*
2. The students will sing *What's the Weather Like Today?*
3. The students will manipulate the names of the school days of the week and types of weather using an interactive chart.
4. The students will read chorally from the interactive chart.
5. The students will create their own verse for the song by using days of the week and types of weather introduced.

MATERIALS: *What's the Weather Like Today?* (big book)
Interactive chart with words of the song printed on it
types of weather cards (cloudy, rainy, windy, snowy, sunny, foggy)
weather pictures
weather video
days-of-the-week cards
paper
pencils
crayons
weather stickers (clouds, rain, wind, snow, sun, fog)

PROCEDURE: The teacher will read *What's the Weather Like Today?* to the students, pointing to words as he or she reads. Students will participate in the reading of the story the second time.

The teacher will introduce the weather terms. A short video depicting the types of weather will be shown. Pictures for each weather term will be displayed. Students will work with the teacher to match the pictures to the correct weather terms.

The teacher will then model singing the song for the students. Students will be invited to sing along while looking at the words.

The teacher will introduce the interactive chart. Students will read the interactive chart with the teacher. The teacher will review the names of the school days of the week. The teacher will then show the words describing different weather types. Students will be asked to describe what it means when the weather is sunny, rainy, windy, and so on. The teacher will put the correct day of the week on the chart. Students will be asked to choose the weather type needed to make the chart true for that day. Students will read the chart. Students will then change the days of the week and the weather types for choral reading by the class. The teacher will display all of the days of the week and all of the weather words on the board. Students will be given paper and a sheet of weather stickers. The students will write their favorite verse for the song choosing their day of the week and weather type. Students will select a sticker to show the weather type. The students will also draw a picture of a day indicative of the weather type selected. Students will work in small groups to share their verses and read together. Each group will choose one work product to share chorally with the class.

ASSESSMENT   Teacher observation and questioning student verses
TOOLS:

What's the weather like Tuesday,

like Tuesday,

like Tuesday?

What's the weather like Tuesday?

Tuesday is sunny!

_____

_____

_____

_____

_____

SUBJECT: SOCIAL STUDIES

PURPOSE: The students will understand that weather forecasts are predictions based upon information and not always completely accurate.

BEHAVIORAL   1. The students will locate the weather page of the newspaper.
OBJECTIVES: 2. The students will discuss the 5-day forecast for the week.
               3. The students will record the 5-day forecast on a recording sheet.
               4. The students will record the actual daily weather underneath the forecasted weather.
               5. The students will evaluate the accuracy of the forecasted weather.

MATERIALS: 1 local newspaper for every two children
               I Can Be a Weather Forecaster
               5-day forecast recording sheets
               taped television weather forecast

PROCEDURE: The teacher will read *I Can Be a Weather Forecaster* to the students. The teacher will explain that the weather forecast can be found in newspapers as well as on television.

               The teacher will show a taped television weather forecast and discuss it. The process of making forecasts will be discussed. The teacher will distribute the newspapers to every other student. Students will be directed to look at the top of the first page to see what they can find that has to do with weather. The teacher will then ask the students how they locate a chapter they want to read in a book (by using the table of contents). The teacher will tell the students that there is something similar to the table of contents on the front page of a newspaper. Students should have the opportunity to look for the directory. Using the directory, students should look to find what page information about the weather can be found.

               Students will then be asked to turn to that page. Students will be given time to determine what kind of information they can find on that page. After being given time to study the weather page, students will be directed to look at the 5-day forecast. The students will discuss the symbols for each day and what they mean. Students will discuss how the forecast could affect some of their activities that week.

Students will record the 5-day forecast on their recording sheets. Each day, students will record the actual weather underneath each forecast. Students will compare the forecasted weather to the actual weather. Students will write observations based upon these comparisons.

ASSESSMENT Teacher observation
TOOLS: Discussion of comparison of forecasted versus actual weather student recording sheets

Weather: Five-Day Forecast

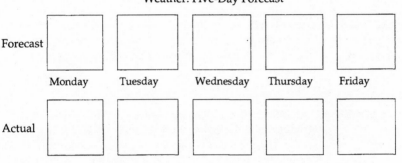

Compare the forecasted weather to the actual weather

_____

_____

_____

_____

_____

_____

SUBJECT: SOCIAL STUDIES

PURPOSE: The students will learn to use maps and map keys.

BEHAVIORAL   1. The students will label the countries of North America.
OBJECTIVES: 2. The students will locate the weather map of the United States
                   in the newspaper.
                3. The students will use the map key of precipitation to describe
                   predicted precipitation for their area.
                4. The students will create a precipitation key for their own map
                   using weather stickers.
                5. The students will place predicted precipitation stickers on
                   areas of the United States map as predicted by the newspaper.

MATERIALS: *Weather Watch*
                   newspapers
                   1 map of North America for each student
                   weather stickers
                   pencils

PROCEDURE: The teacher will read *Weather Watch* to the students as an
                   introduction to the lesson. Students will be asked to locate the
                   weather page of the newspaper using the method introduced in
                   the previous social studies lesson. The teacher will direct the
                   students' attention to the precipitation map key and explain its
                   meaning.

                   The teacher will give each student a map of North America. The
                   teacher will help the students identify and label the countries of
                   North America. Students will be asked to locate the map of the
                   United States in the newspaper and name some of the precipitation
                   predictions they see for that day. Students will point out the
                   general location where they live in the United States and name
                   the predicted precipitation for their area.

                   Students will create their own precipitation map key using
                   corresponding weather stickers to represent the precipitation
                   predictions for areas of the United States that day on their own
                   maps.

ASSESSMENT   Teacher observation
TOOLS: Student maps and map keys

SUBJECT: SCIENCE

PURPOSE: The students will learn the following cloud types: cirrus, stratus, cumulus, and nimbus.

The students will state what type of weather is associated with each cloud type.

BEHAVIORAL   1. The students will identify different cloud types.
OBJECTIVES: 2. The students will photograph cloud types.
3. The students will illustrate the cloud types present on the day of the lesson.
4. The students will decide what type of weather each cloud type brings.
5. The students will create a cloud type using cotton balls or other art media.
6. The students will judge the art projects for accurately portraying the cloud type intended.

MATERIALS: Tomie de Paola's *Cloud Book*
pictures of cirrus, stratus, cumulus, and nimbus clouds
blue paper
crayons
glue
cotton balls
1 instant camera
chart listing cloud types

PROCEDURE: The teacher will read Tomie de Paola's *Cloud Book* to the class, focusing on the different types of clouds and what they mean in terms of the weather. Students will then be taken outside to observe clouds. The students will be divided into four groups. Each group will use an instant camera to photograph the clouds present that day. Students will lie on their backs to observe the clouds. Crayons and paper can be used for the students to illustrate what they see in the sky. The students will discuss with their group which type of cloud they see in the sky and what type of weather is associated with this type of cloud.

Once in the classroom, the teacher will show the class pictures of the different cloud types. The students will identify the cloud types in the pictures. The students will than attach their photographs of clouds under the appropriate name on the chart.

Students will pick their favorite cloud type and create it using cotton balls, crayons, paper, glue, and other art media. Students will write a sentence on their art project about the type of weather their cloud brings. The students will share their creations. The class will try to properly identify the cloud type creations.

ASSESSMENT TOOLS:　Teacher observation and questioning
Projects created by students
Oral participation of students in evaluating projects

FOLLOW-UP:　Students will photograph and identify cloud types on different days throughout the unit. The students will place the photographs under the appropriate cloud name on the chart.

SUBJECT: LANGUAGE ARTS/SCIENCE

PURPOSE:　The students will learn what wind is and what it can do.

BEHAVIORAL OBJECTIVES:
1. The students will recall factual information.
2. The students will repeat things the wind can do after listening to *Feel the Wind*.
3. The students will name other things that the wind can do.
4. The students will write four things that the wind can do on a pinwheel pattern.
5. The students will construct a pinwheel.
6. The students will blow on their pinwheels in order to make them move.
7. The students will write in their journals the most important thing they learned about wind.

MATERIALS:　pinwheel patterns
Feel the Wind
1 pencil per student for pinwheels
1 straight pin or tack per student
pencils for writing
journals
chart paper

PROCEDURE:　The teacher will read *Feel the Wind* to the students. The students will discuss what wind is and what it can do as the reading goes on.

The students will work in groups to write on chart paper the things the wind can do. The students will be encouraged to list

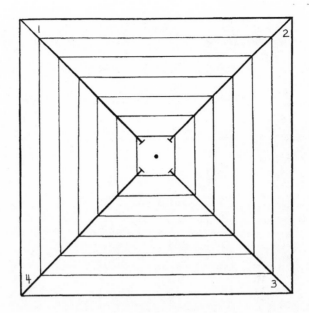

things that were in the book and things that were not in the book. The students will individually write four important things wind can do on a pinwheel pattern. The students will exchange papers with a neighbor. The neighbor will read to determine whether or not the wind can do the things listed. The teacher will monitor group work, individual work, and partner work.

The teacher will demonstrate how to make a pinwheel using the pattern, a pencil, and a straight pin. Students will make their pinwheels and use their "wind" power to make them work.

Students will review what they learned about the capabilities of wind and write in their journals what they think the most important capability is and why they think so.

ASSESSMENT   Teacher observation
TOOLS: Written responses on pinwheel patterns
                Written responses in journals

Directions: Cut out square. Cut each diagonal to the dash. Fold in all numbered corners. Push a thumbtack through points one through four. Push tack through center of the pinwheel. Push tack into the eraser of a pencil to complete pinwheel.

SUBJECT: SCIENCE/MATH

PURPOSE: The students will learn to use a thermometer to complete a
                scientific experiment.

BEHAVIORAL   1. The students will listen to an introduction to sun and
OBJECTIVES: temperature.
             2. The students will make a hypothesis about the effects of the
                sun on the temperature of water.
             3. The students will accurately read a thermometer (Fahrenheit
                scale).
             4. The students will record the results of the effects of the sun
                on the temperature of water.
             5. The students will evaluate the accuracy of their hypothesis.

MATERIALS: demonstration thermometer
                large outdoor thermometer
                12 small thermometers
                12 small, plastic containers
                water
                2 large construction paper ovals (exactly the same size)
                per student for pop-up dioramas

Focus on Weather and Climate
markers
four 3 × 5 index cards per student
construction paper scraps
glue
scissors

PROCEDURE: The students will be taken outside. They will be directed to stand
in the sun for a few minutes. Then they will be directed to stand
in the shade for a few minutes. The students will be asked to
discuss their observations, to compare the way their skin felt in
the sun and in the shade. The students will also be asked to feel
a blacktop surface in both the sun and the shade and share their
observations.

The students will be divided into six groups. Each group will be
given two small plastic containers. The containers should be
filled halfway with water. Students will be directed to go outside to place one container in direct sunlight and one container
in the shade.

Once back inside, the teacher will read pages 14 to 15 of *Focus
on Weather and Climate* to the students to provide background
information about the sun and temperature. The teacher will ask
the students what is used to measure temperature. The teacher
will introduce the demonstration thermometer and large outdoor
thermometer and describe how a thermometer works. The teacher
will let the students know that a larger number means a higher
temperature and a smaller number means a lower temperature.
Students should be given the opportunity to study the two
thermometers. The teacher will show examples of how to read
the thermometer using the Fahrenheit scale. Students will be asked
to read the temperature shown on the demonstration thermometer. Students will then take turns setting the temperature on the
thermometer and selecting other students to read the temperature.

The students will be asked to think about the temperature of the
water in the containers placed outside previously. They will be
asked to form a hypothesis about the temperature of the water
in the two containers. Will the temperatures be the same or
different? If different, which temperature will be higher? Students
will be asked to record their hypothesis by completing one
portion of a diorama to illustrate their hypothesis. Students
will share their hypothesis with the class.

Following this, students will go outside to check the temperature of water in each container using thermometers. The students will be asked to write down their results. The results will be discussed within the group.

Once back inside, the teacher will ask the students to share their group's results. The teacher will write the temperatures for each container of each group on the board. Students will discuss the patterns they see in each group's results and why the results turned out that way.

Students will then record the results of their study on the remaining part of the diorama.

When this is completed, the students will open their journals and evaluate the accuracy of their own hypothesis as compared with the results. They will also write a paragraph describing how to use a thermometer.

ASSESSMENT   Teacher observation of children using thermometers
TOOLS: Dioramas
                  Journals

SUBJECT: PHONICS

PURPOSE: The students will review the short and long vowel sounds.

BEHAVIORAL   1. The students will recall the different vowel sounds.
OBJECTIVES: 2. The students will review words having the different vowel
                     sounds.
                  3. The students will give examples of words having the different
                     vowel sounds.
                  4. The students will search for words having **short a, e, i, o, u**
                     and **long a, e, i, o, u** in *White Snow, Bright Snow*.
                  5. The students will exchange recording sheets with a partner
                     to check for correct answers on recording sheets.

MATERIALS: multiple copies of *White Snow, Bright Snow*
                  vowel search recording sheets
                  chalkboard
                  chalk
                  pencils

PROCEDURE: The teacher will lead the class to recall the sounds made by vowels. The teacher will give an example of a word containing each vowel sound. He or she will write these words under the appropriate headings on the chalkboard.

The students will then be asked to give words containing vowel sounds to add to the list on the chalkboard. The teacher will read *White Snow, Bright Snow* to the class. Students should discuss the story. The teacher will then read the story again, this time asking the students to focus on words having the vowel sounds that are being learned. After reading the first two pages, the teacher will ask the students to find words and identify their vowel sounds. After several examples from the book have been completed, the teacher will give the students a vowel search recording sheet.

The students will work in small groups with a copy of the book *White Snow, Bright Snow* to find words for each vowel sound and write the words in the appropriate place. When completed, the students will exchange papers with members of another group for checking. Students will provide feedback to each other regarding the accuracy of their work.

ASSESSMENT
TOOLS:
Teacher observation and questioning
Vowel search recording sheets

VOWEL SEARCH

Title of Book or Poem: _____

Author: _____

short a   long a

short e   long e

short i   long i

short o   long o

short u   long u

SUBJECT: MATH

PURPOSE: The students will learn to use pattern blocks to copy simple designs and to create designs of their own.

OBJECTIVES: 1. The students will copy a simple design.
               2. The students will alter the design to make it their own.
               3. The students will demonstrate how to make a weather design using pattern blocks.
               4. The students will use pattern blocks to make another weather shape.
               5. The students will give an award for the best weather shape.

MATERIALS: pattern blocks (wooden or plastic)
               pattern block stickers or cutout shapes
               construction paper
               glue

PROCEDURE: Ask the students to look at weather designs you have created with pattern block shapes. Demonstrate how to look at these shapes and recreate them using pattern block stickers or cutout shapes.

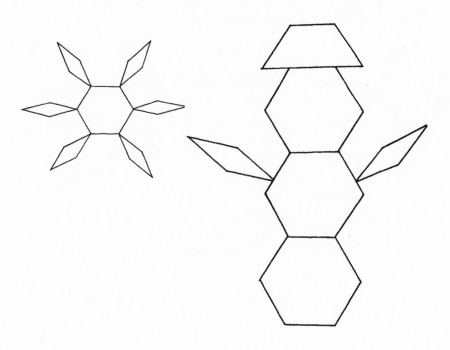

Students should be given pattern blocks and asked to recreate the given shapes (snowman, cloud, sun, etc.). Students should then be asked to change something about the picture. Students will be asked to demonstrate making a design using the pattern blocks. Students will represent their shapes on paper using the pattern block stickers or cutouts.

Brainstorm other weather pictures the students might create using pattern blocks. Have the students use pattern blocks and then pattern block stickers or cutouts to make their own weather designs on construction paper.

Students can decide which weather designs will receive a special reward for creativity or be placed in a class book.

ASSESSMENT TOOLS: Teacher observation
Designs made on construction paper using pattern block stickers or cutouts

---

SUBJECT: LANGUAGE ARTS

PURPOSE: The students will write a story to demonstrate their understanding of problems and solutions.

OBJECTIVES:
1. The students will list good and bad things the weather can cause to happen.
2. The students will write a story incorporating the good and bad things weather can cause.
3. The students will share their stories with the class.
4. The students will each write a letter to a fellow student letting the student know what they liked about his or her story.

MATERIALS: construction paper
teacher example of a story
chart paper
markers
scissors
glue

PROCEDURE:　The teacher will put a chart on the board and ask students to think about types of weather and good and bad things the weather can cause. The teacher will record the students' responses on the chart.

The teacher will define *problem* and *solution*. The teacher will give examples of problems and solutions from stories read earlier in class. The teacher will let the students know that he or she would like the students to write an adventure for a character, showing how weather affected the character's choices, problems, and solutions. The teacher will share several examples with the class, modeling what he or she wants.

Students will be directed to use some of the responses given on the chart as well as to incorporate some of their own ideas to show problems and solutions for the main character.

Materials will be distributed. When students have completed their stories, time will be provided to read the stories to the class.

Students will each write a letter to a friend letting the friend know what they liked about their friend's story.

ASSESSMENT　Teacher observation and questioning
TOOLS:　Charted responses
　　　　Student stories

Luckily
one sunny day Jeremy got invited to the beach.

Unluckily
it began to rain.

Luckily
Jeremy found a beach umbrella.

Unluckily
the wind blew the umbrella away.

THEME AS A GIFT

You may wish to give gifts to your teammates or, later in your career, to a student teacher whom you will guide. It is a wonderful thing to give a teammate or a student teacher a teaching unit that you have developed. Every teacher enjoys a creative, ready-to-use packet of activities.

For example, perhaps you have the opportunity and time to create a theme that has not been used on your grade level. You choose to create a theme about Treasure Seekers. The gift can be given to each member of your team. The gift could include map activities, seek-a-word puzzles, literature activities, a bibliography of books that could be used, treasure-seeking poems, and so on. You could also include an inexpensive book or coloring book related to the theme for each teacher. All of the items could be bundled together with wide ribbon, decorated with a sack of candy coins, and personalized with a note from you. You could give these gifts during the holiday season or at the end of the year.

Teachers and student teachers not only will have a gift, but also some ready-to-use activities that could be used when needed. You will get so much enjoyment out of developing and sharing this gift. You will be providing a thoughtful gift for your friends while developing new activities for your own students. It is definitely a win-win situation!

7

Instructional Presentation

Good instructional presentation is very important to student success. Students need to have information presented in a clear, easily understood manner. Like a good story, an instructional lesson needs a strong beginning, middle, and ending. Throughout the lesson, students need opportunities to be involved actively, rather than passively, in the learning.

This chapter will highlight major elements necessary in the beginning, middle, and ending of a strong instructional lesson. Following descriptors of these elements, an example of their use will be given pertaining to a lesson used in a primary classroom. The objective of the lesson is that the students will match objects to number words. The teacher knows that in order for students to successfully achieve this objective, they must have the prerequisite knowledge of being able to read the number words independently.

BEGINNING

At the beginning of your lesson, you need to let the students know what the outcome of the lesson will be. This will be the time to state the learning objective. Once you have stated the learning objective, let the students know what work they will complete to demonstrate that they have mastered the objective.

You will need to ask students to recall any prior learning necessary for mastering this lesson's information. Review the prior information by asking questions to check for understanding. If students do not have the prerequisite knowledge, you will have difficulty building upon it.

It is helpful to use a relevant piece of literature as an introduction to your lessons. In almost every subject area, dealing with any learning objective, you can now find a piece of children's literature related to your subject of study.

> *Teacher:* Boys and Girls, today we are going to make counting books using bears. When we make our counting books, we are going to match the number words *one* through *ten* to the correct number of bears. We are then going to write sentences or a story for each page in our counting books.

> On your desk, you will find a bag containing cards with number words written on them. We are going to begin by playing a game with these word cards. Spread the word cards on your desk so that you can see each card. See how I have spread my word cards out on the blackboard?

> Now, we are going to play the number game. I want to see how quickly you can find the word *eight*. Once you have found the word *eight*, raise your hand. I am going to count to eight. When I get to eight, I want everyone to hold up the word *eight* to show me.

This can be repeated with different numbers until the teacher is convinced that the majority of the students have demonstrated mastery of the prerequisite skill. Variations of the game can be used by having students select the numbers. Through this review, students are already actively involved through working with their word cards.

> *Teacher:* Boys and Girls, you have done a super job with playing the number game. Now I would like for you to put your number cards back into the bags and join me on the carpet for a counting story about bears.

The teacher reads *Numbears* by Kathleen Hague to the students. The teacher and students discuss the story as they read. The teacher points out the number words in the story and has the children count the number of bears on each page.

MIDDLE

Once you have introduced the lesson, you will need to present needed information and skills. While presenting information, get students involved as much as possible. Use different strategies such as questioning, having volunteers assist you, allowing students to use manipulatives, and so on throughout your instructional presentation.

Direct the students through the steps of what you would like them to accomplish. If the students will be required to make a work product, work with the students to create one or two work products similar to what they will be creating.

Once the students have shown, through their work with you, that they are ready to complete an instructional task independently, show an example of your own, detailing exactly what you expect of their work product. Your concrete example will set the standard for your students and give a visual account of your expectations.

> *Teacher:* Now that we have read *Numbears*, we will complete an activity together to match the bears with the correct number words. I have on this table the stuffed teddy bears you have brought from home. I am going to put a word card on the blackboard. This word is *three*. I am going to select three bears from the table to match with the word card. Lets try again. This time I am going to use the word *t-e-n*. Raise your hand if you can read this number word.

> Yes, *ten* is correct. I need a volunteer to go to the bear table to select ten bears to match with the word card *ten*.

This activity is repeated until many students have had the opportunity to participate.

> Boys and girls, you have done such a great job with the stuffed bears that now I want to try another activity. Get out the word cards that we used earlier. Also get out the teddy bear counters that were passed out earlier.

> I want you to arrange the number words in order going down your desks as I have arranged mine on the board. I then want you to count the correct number of teddy bear counters to place next to each number word. Look at the board to see that next to the word *five*, I have placed five teddy bear counters. Work until you have matched all of the word cards with the correct number of teddy bear counters. I will be walking around to see how you are doing. Raise your hand if you need any help.

> I am so pleased with how well you completed that activity. I think it is now time for us to make our counting books. Place your teddy bear counters on the tray in the middle of your table.

> I am passing out a blank book and a bag of cutout bears for each of you. These are materials you will need to make your counting books.

I want you to think about the book *Numbears*. You are now going to make your own "numbears" books by using what we have worked with today.

I have already made two different books that I'd like to share with you. I made these books using number word cards like the ones you have at your desk and teddy bear cutouts.

The teacher shares her two books. The first one is aimed at her beginning readers and writers. The book matches the number words and bears on each page in sequential order. Backgrounds have been drawn on each book page. The text the teacher has added is as follows:

I see one red bear.
I see two yellow bears.
I see three brown bears.
I see four green bears.
I see five black bears.
I see six orange bears.
I see seven blue bears.
I see eight purple bears.
I see nine white bears.
I see ten pink bears.

The second teacher-made example was made with higher-level readers and writers in mind. The book was made just like the first example. Only the text is different. The text of the second book is as follows:

One red bear is resting in the sun.
Two yellow bears are having some fun.
Three brown bears are riding their bikes.
Four green bears are flying yellow kites.
Five blue bears are tying their shoes.
Six orange bears are looking for clues.
Seven blue bears are trying to eat.
Eight purple bears are crossing the street.
Nine white bears are singing a song.
Ten pink bears are humming along.

After sharing the two examples with the class, the teacher lets the students know which elements will be necessary in each student book. The teacher lets the students know that everyone must match the number words and bears in sequential order on each page. The teacher may also require that a background be drawn on each page and that some writing accompany the illustrations.

The teacher will then let the students know that once they meet the above criteria, they can be as creative as they want with the writing. Some students may even wish to try to use rhyming words in their stories, pattern their writing after the first example, or make their stories using their own idea.

In this manner, students are not only demonstrating their knowledge of the skill, they are bringing in other content areas (writing, language arts) to use while working on the skill. This work product allows flexibility for differing academic abilities and opens the door for student creativity.

ENDING

In the conclusion of your lesson, prior to student independent work, you need to check for students' understanding of the material presented and that they have met your expectations for student independent work. This can be accomplished by questioning the students. Ask students specific questions or ask for volunteers to describe for the class what they are to do.

If, through questioning, the teacher is satisfied that the majority of the class fully understands the material and tasks to be completed, the teacher should let the students begin the independent work. If, through questioning, the teacher determines that the majority of students do not understand the information well enough to be successful with the assignment, he or she will need to present the information in a different manner or give further examples to assure student success. Through questioning, the teacher may also pinpoint certain individuals who will need further assistance. These individuals can be worked with separately while the rest of the class works independently.

While the students are working independently, the teacher will need to walk among the students to make sure they are succeeding with the instructional task. The teacher can assist any students experiencing difficulty with the task.

At the conclusion of the independent work time, students can share their work products with the class, and the teacher can use this time to reiterate the main points from the lesson. The work products can be collected to be graded and assessed for individual student understanding.

> *Teacher:* Boys and Girls, I would like a volunteer to tell the class
> what you need to do in your booklets.

The teacher will listen to volunteers to determine whether the students fully understand the assignment. This will also give the listening students another chance to hear the directions. The teacher will probe until all necessary information has been discussed and repeated.

The students will begin working on making their counting books using the supplied materials. The teacher will monitor the class while students complete the independent work. Any student experiencing difficulty or needing additional support will be given assistance during this time.

Once students have finished the assignment, they will be given the opportunity to read their counting books to the class and share their illustrations. This sharing of work will reinforce the learning of the skill while giving students the benefit of seeing how their classmates creatively displayed the information.

Presenting information in a meaningful, active, and sequential manner will keep students involved in the learning. It will also allow students to be more successful in achieving the objectives you have to set for them. If you have done your part, the students will be sure to do their part.

8

Differentiation of Instruction

In any given classroom you will find students of varying ability levels. Often, in one classroom, you will find students working on three different grade levels. In a typical first-grade classroom, you will have students who have not yet achieved kindergarten objectives, students ready for first-grade work, and students who need the challenges of a second-grade curriculum. It will be your job to make sure you are adequately challenging and meeting the needs of all your students. Each child needs to make 1 year's growth from the point he or she enters the classroom.

If the teacher of the above mentioned first-grade class simply taught a straight first-grade lesson, the children needing to master kindergarten skills would be lost. Those students requiring second-grade work would become bored. Assigning work that does not meet the needs of all of your students is one of the best ways to invite disorder and discipline problems. It is not too difficult to meet the needs of every student in your classroom.

There are several ways to differentiate instruction to meet the needs of all the students in your classroom. This can be achieved by layering assignments, by grouping students into ability and skills groups, and by using learning centers.

LAYERING ASSIGNMENTS

Assignments can be layered so that you have different expectations on assignments for different students. For example, if your teaching objective is to have students recall in sequential order what happens first, next, then, and last in a story, you could have the students complete the objective on differing layers using a book about butterflies. After reading the literature selection about butterflies to the students, pass out butterfly-shaped booklets to each student. Each butterfly booklet should have four pages with the words *first, next, then,* and *last* already written on them. For the group of students working with mastering kindergarten skills, you would expect them to draw pictures of what happened first, next, then, and last in the story. Once they have completed this, these students could dictate a sentence to you for each page. Students could help you sound out the words as you are writing their dictation. The group working on grade level could write their own sentence for each page and illustrate their writing. The group requiring second-grade work could write a paragraph on each page of their butterfly books. Once you have presented the lesson to the entire class and given basic instructions, you could have the students illustrate the front cover of their butterfly booklets as you call each group respectively to give more specific instructions of your expectations for what they should do in their books.

After completing this type of layering several times, students will begin to make their own choices regarding what type of work they should be doing on assignments. Students should always be encouraged to do their very best and to work to their maximum potential. If you notice a student who is working below his or her capabilities, have a conference with the student to let him or her know what you expect of his or her work. You may even find through this type of layering that the lower-achieving students try to stretch themselves to mirror the work of the higher-achieving students.

Just make sure that you always have the highest expectations of every student. Once you know what individuals are capable of, you will know what reasonable expectations and levels of support are needed for each student. In this way, you can nurture all of your students and push them to the next level of academic development without overwhelming them.

GROUPING

Providing small group instruction in your classroom will be one of the most valuable ways to differentiate instruction to meet the needs of all of your students. Small group instruction can be used for any subject area. Small group instruction is most commonly found in reading instruction. There are challenges to teaching small groups in the classroom. These challenges include forming appropriate groups of children, planning activities for small group instruction, and managing the rest of the class while working with small groups.

Two main ways to group children for small groups are to group children with similar abilities in a specific area and to group children needing instruction on a particular skill. Groups with children sharing similar abilities will change less frequently than groups of children needing instruction on certain skills.

However you choose to group your students, always maintain assessment records pertaining to abilities and mastery of skills. In this way, students needing to be moved to another group will have the opportunity to do so. You should never keep the same groupings throughout an entire school year. Children's ability and skill levels change tremendously throughout an academic year. Your groupings need to reflect these changes.

In reading, you may decide that you want all students placed in groups to read materials on their instructional reading level. After assessing the students, you may find that you have three distinct groupings of ability levels.

Perhaps your class has been working on the theme of outer space. You want all students reading books related to the theme in your reading groups. You have noticed that your class has been having difficulty sequencing events in a story. You decide that you would like to teach a sequencing lesson to each reading group using appropriately leveled materials. You might use a book about the moon that contains very little text and many picture clues for the group that is not yet reading on a first-grade level. The first-grade readers might complete the sequencing activity with an easy reader about astronauts. The group reading on a second-grade level might work with a chapter book about the planets of the solar system to complete the sequencing activity. In this manner, all students in your classroom can work with materials on their instructional level that pertain to your classroom theme of study to complete the skill lesson.

In this same classroom, you may see that the reading groups need not only be working with materials on their instructional reading level but also be working on different skills in order to make progress with their reading abilities. You can select materials for each instructional reading level pertaining to your overall theme of study and plan different types of activities for the reading groups. Let's say that at this point of the year, your students are working with the weather theme.

Following the descriptions of activities pertaining to weather that are planned for each group, you will find the instructional activities used for these groups.

Perhaps you have noticed that your beginning readers are in need of practice rereading selections and matching the text of the story with the pictures. You copy the text and pictures from a book. You have selected the book *Why?* by Miriam Frost because it is the correct reading level and has a portion in it about the color of clouds. You allow students, after reading the book under your direction, to match each sentence of the book with the picture that goes with the sentence. As an independent follow-up activity, you give each student a copy of the text from the story and a booklet. You direct the students to cut out the sentences, glue them on a page in their booklet, and properly illustrate each sentence. To extend the learning activity, those students up for the challenge can create two additional pages for the story by following the story format.

You have noticed weaknesses with the first-grade readers with recalling factual information to answer comprehension questions. For this group, you have selected a nonfiction book titled *Umbrellas* by Suzanne Lilly. After reading *Umbrellas* with this group, you will work with the students to answer comprehension questions that you have developed.

For the students reading on a second-grade level, you have covered quite a bit of information and would like an informal assessment of their mastery. You select the book *Storm!* by Diana Noonan because it is the proper reading level for this group and ties into the theme of weather. You direct students to read portions of this chapter book independently and complete the corresponding parts of the packet to check their understanding of base words, syllables in words, writing chapter summaries, and so on. By checking completed packets, you will be able to determine areas needing more work.

(The following activities, based on the books *Why?* by Miriam Frost, *Umbrellas* by Suzanne Lilly, and *Storm!* by Diana Noonan, are used with permission from The Wright Group, 19201 120th Avenue NE, Bothell, Washington 98011, 1-800-523-2371.)

 **Why?**

by Miriam Frost

Why are clouds white but not green?

Why do we ride horses but not zebras?

Why do dogs bark but not cats?

Why do boats float but not sink?

Why is snow cold but not warm?

Why do we fall down but not up?

Why do bats sleep upside down but not right side up?

Why do we stand on our feet but not on our hands?

1. Write two more lines for this story on your own.

_____

_____

_____

_____

Umbrellas

by Suzanne Lilly

1. Where were umbrellas invented?

_____

2. What were the first umbrellas made of?

_____

3. What are two elements of weather that umbrellas protect against?

_____

4. The first umbrellas were made with a little _____

hanging on the handle. People thought the acorn would protect against

_____.

5. What fact did you find most interesting in this book?

_____

_____

Storm!

by Diana Noonan

CHAPTER 1

1. Write the base word for each of the following words from Chapter 1.

blinked   _____

pulled   _____

rumbling   _____

whispered   _____

awakened   _____

appeared   _____

looking   _____

battling   _____

flickering   _____

burning   _____

2. Sam was worried about something in this chapter. Describe what Sam was worried about.

_____

_____

_____

_____

CHAPTER 2

1. How is Dandy-lion trapped?

_____

_____

2. What did the rain cause Sam to do as he looked for Dandy-lion?

_____

_____

3. How is Sam feeling throughout this chapter?

_____

_____

_____

CHAPTER 3

1. How is Dandy-lion trapped?

_____

2. How did Dad and Sam get to the cliff?

_____

3. What do you think will happen next?

_____

CHAPTER 4

1. Write a summary for Chapter 4.

_____

_____

_____

2. How was Sam feeling throughout this chapter? Why?

_____

_____

_____

CHAPTER 5

1. Complete the following vowel search:

short a _____   long a _____

short e _____   long e _____

short i _____   long i _____

short o _____   long o _____

short u _____   long u _____

CHAPTER 6

1. Find a rhyming word in Chapter 6 for each of the following words:

lightened _____

Dave _____

gown _____

cried _____

burning _____

scrubbed _____

whiff _____

spying _____

hollow _____

thief _____

2. What is the main idea of this chapter?

_____

_____

CHAPTER 7

1. How many syllables are in each of the following words from Chapter 7?

tractor _____   travel _____

current _____   perched _____

reef _____   anything _____

attention _____   window _____

2. Why were the characters excited at the end of Chapter 7?

_____

_____

CHAPTER 8

1. Once Dandy-lion was safely on shore, what more did the main characters have to worry about?

_____

_____

_____

2. Do you think Dandy-lion will be well again? Why or why not?

_____

_____

_____

CHAPTER 9

1. Why didn't Dad want Sam checking on Dandy-lion?

_____

2. What was the weather like during this chapter?

_____

CHAPTER 10

1. What was the surprise in Chapter 10?

_____

_____

_____

_____

CENTERS

Learning centers are an important aspect of any primary classroom. Learning centers provide an excellent avenue for differentiating work for students. Learning centers encourage teamwork, responsibility, and choice. Learning centers can be used after students finish their regular classroom work or as an activity to be done while you are working with a reading or other small instructional group.

It is essential that centers are well planned, well organized, and well supervised. Learning centers will require much effort and supervision for the first weeks of implementation. Once you have established your routine and expectations, center time will begin to run smoothly.

If you plan to use learning centers for activities students can do during group instructional times, you will need to make sure that the students understand that the noise level during center time must be kept to a bare minimum. These center activities need to be planned so students can complete them independently. Use your normal discipline procedures when introducing center activities. Some students may have a difficult time adapting to such freedom of choice, as they might not have experienced such freedoms in prior school situations. You will need to work with these students to help them understand how to work appropriately in centers. In the first days of implementation, you may even need to let some students know that if they make excessive noise in the centers and have to be repeatedly spoken to, they will have to go to time out for the remainder of center time for that day. In most instances, this will have to be done only once to show the students that you mean what you say.

Your center activities will change from week to week or from theme to theme. You may wish to have several centers that are consistent throughout the school year. Some easy centers to maintain throughout the year are a listening center, a filmstrip center, and an art center. The centers remain the same. It is the materials provided in these centers that will need to be changed.

The listening center can contain books with tapes related to your themes to be listened to using headphones. Books should represent a variety of reading levels. You can also include tapes of songs in your listening center. Provide the words for students to read while they listen to the songs. Students love to listen to stories and songs of their choice. Keep in mind that some of your students might not have access to books or audio books in their homes. Demonstrate to students how to operate and take care of the equipment and materials in this center. Students of all abilities will enjoy this center.

If your school media center or library has a filmstrip projector available, check it out for use in your classroom. Students love to view filmstrips related to the theme of study. As a follow-up activity for this center, provide students with a worksheet of filmstrip frames. Have students draw and write in the filmstrip frames about three things they learned by watching the filmstrip.

In the art center, students can work with art media to create a project related to your theme of study. Some weeks you may wish to have all the students make a specific project. For example, if working with an outer space theme, you might have all the students create an outer space rocket ship using the materials provided in the center. Students will all be working to make the same project, but creativity will be expected. Other weeks you may direct students to make any project of their choosing related to the theme of study. Or you can always let students create any project they wish, whether it is related to the theme or not.

Some centers, such as a language arts center and a mathematics center, will require more time and planning on your part. You will need to plan activities for these centers dealing with your theme and your focus of study in these academic areas. For example, if you are working on an outer space theme and initial consonant sounds in language arts, you might put a matching game in the language arts center. In this game, students can take aliens with pictures of different objects on their tummies and place them in the spaceship with the correct initial consonant letter. The students would need to place aliens with the cat, coat, and cow on their tummies in the spaceship labeled with the letter c, and would need to place the aliens with the mountain, moose, and moat on their tummies in the spaceship labeled with the letter m, and so on. You could either make this center self-checking by providing an answer key or have the students record their responses on a worksheet that could be checked by you at a later time. The worksheet could consist of photocopies of aliens and space ships. Students could cut out the aliens and glue them onto the correct space ships.

In mathematics, your focus of study might be fractions. Again with the outer space theme, students could match space ships or planets divided into fractional pieces with the correct fraction. This activity could also be tailored to be either self- or teacher checked.

It is often more meaningful if you have some way to check the work completed by your students in centers. You will need to know that your students are completing the assignments accurately and that center time is being used wisely. If you have centers that are self-checking, make sure to vary from week to week with center work that will be checked by you.

Many teachers use some form of center contract to help monitor the center activities students have completed. A center contract will list the centers available. The teacher, teaching assistant, or student will mark with a check, sticker, or the like, each center he or she has completed.

Another management system for centers is to provide all necessary supplies for each center in a folder marked with the student's name. At the beginning of each week or theme, the students will receive their folders with all materials needed for center work for that week or theme. Throughout the center working times, each student will need to keep all completed assignments in his or her folder. During and at the completion of the week or theme, you can check each child's center folder for completed work. In this way, you can easily keep up with how children are using their center time and collect completed work for review and grading.

Learning centers are a wonderful way to provide exciting choices for your students for academic reinforcement and enrichment. Learning centers can be planned for any of the subject areas. Each center in your classroom can be planned with several choices of activities to accommodate different ability levels of your students. Although planning for centers can be time-consuming, the time is well spent. Your students will always look forward to working in learning centers if the centers are relevant, engaging, and can be completed independently.

9

Student Assessment and Record Keeping

Maintaining accurate records and keeping up with student performance is a very important aspect of teaching. This chapter gives information regarding how to create and maintain student portfolios, how to set up and maintain a grade book, and how to complete report cards and report card comments. It also gives advice pertaining to grading daily student class work and homework assignments.

CREATING STUDENT PORTFOLIOS

Student portfolios should contain pieces of student work and teacher assessments that show the growth the student demonstrates throughout the school year. The first samples in the portfolio should show skills and proficiencies the student has upon entering your classroom. The last samples should show ending skills and proficiencies on grade-level-and-above materials. Portfolios will be sent to the students' future teachers and may be used for accountability purposes. Check into your school and district guidelines regarding student portfolios and portfolio contents.

At the beginning of the year, it is a good idea to assess students in reading, writing, and mathematics. Your reading assessment might be done to find the child's instructional reading level. Your math assessment might be a test of skills the child should have mastered in the previous school year as well as skills that should be covered this school year. For the writing assessment, you could have the children write about a specific topic or prompt. Make sure to date all materials when placing them in the portfolio. Include relevant comments and feedback on portfolio contents.

As the year goes on, choose materials you feel are relevant for assessing the child's progress each grading period to be included in the portfolio. You may always include more information in the student portfolio than end-of-grading-period information. At the end of the year, you can sort through student portfolios to determine which contents should remain in the portfolio for future teachers.

Allow the students to select several pieces of their work to be included in the portfolio. Have the student write on the work why he or she selected it to be included in the portfolio.

Your end-of-the-year assessment data will be the final addition to the student portfolio. Take the time to compare the students' end-of-year assessments with the beginning-of-the-year assessments. You will be amazed by the growth that is evident.

Portfolios are a tremendous help to teachers on the next grade level. Portfolios also demonstrate the growth the child has had while under your guidance in your classroom. Portfolio contents can also be helpful when trying to get services for children with special needs. This written documentation of regularly assessed student performance will aid in the decision-making process for gaining special education services for children requiring these services. Student portfolio contents can be a tremendous help when conferencing with a student's parents.

You can use student portfolio contents when completing report cards. The portfolio contents will give concrete evidence of mastery of skills. The portfolio contents will also easily lead you to specific, meaningful report card comments to assist the parents and the students.

Whether or not your school district or school requires maintaining student portfolios, you should start your portfolios as soon as the year begins. These documents will contain valuable information to help you, your students, their parents, and your colleagues.

SETTING UP AND MAINTAINING GRADE BOOKS

Grade books are generally provided for teachers by the school. You will need to set up your grade book in a manner that will be easy for you to use and maintain. Before setting up your grade book, get a copy of the report card for your school. Enter subjects in the same order as they appear on the report card. This will enable you to complete report cards more easily at the end of each grading period.

Once you have determined the order in which to list the subjects, be sure to designate a page for each grading period for each subject. If your school system operates on four 9-week grading periods, designate four pages for each subject. Affixing colorful, plastic tabs to the first page of each subject will enable you to turn to areas in your grade book quickly.

Once you have all graded areas labeled and tabbed, you may wish to designate pages of your grade book for homework, attendance, and checklists. The checklists can be used for marking names of children who have purchased school insurance, have brought in picture money, or have turned in the necessary permission slips for class trips. Checklists can also be used to keep up with student work as it is turned in.

It is a good guideline to enter at least one grade per subject per week. When possible, use numerical grading systems. Numerical grading systems are much less likely to be disputed than subjective grading systems. Clearly, a student answering 8 out of 10 questions on an assessment would receive a grade of 80%. You will need to determine which assignments should be given grades that will be recorded in your grade book. At the end of each grading period, simply average the grades to determine the child's mark on the report card. Most school districts will offer guidelines to designate specific grades for ranges of numerical grades.

Numerical grades can easily be averaged using a spreadsheet program. You may also wish to invest in software specifically designed for entering and averaging grades. Table 9.1 is an example of a page of numerical grades for mathematics for one 9-week grading period. Notice that the grade-book page is set up to allow finding the date of each test given and the subject areas the test covered.

COMPLETING REPORT CARDS

Completion of report cards is often a task many teachers look upon with dread. Report cards can be time-consuming due to making meaningful comments about each child. Don't ever procrastinate when it comes to report card completion. The longer you put off the task, the more grueling it will become. It is often easier to break up report cards into separate tasks.

You might start working on your report cards by averaging the grades in specific subjects. Once the grades have been averaged, you will be able to assign grades in each subject area and enter these grades on report cards. Be sure to follow your school and school district guidelines when assigning grades.

Report card comments will be more helpful and meaningful if you include at least three major points. Your report card comments should begin with a positive comment for each child. You will need to find at least one great thing to share with the parents regarding their child. For example, *John is an enthusiastic learner who readily participates in classroom discussions*. Or, *Sarah has excelled with mathematical concepts and objectives this term*.

The next portion of your comment should pertain to something the child needs to work on in order to improve in some area. No matter how advanced a student may be, there is always an area or two that can be focused on for necessary growth. As

Table 9.1

Math Grades For Second 9-Week Grading Period

DATE SUBJECT		1/15 FACTS TO 18	1/22 FACT FAMILIES	1/29 PLACE VALUE	2/4 PLACE VALUE	2/11 INCHES	2/18 CM	2/25 TIME	3/4 TIME	3/5 CUMULATIVE	2nd GRADING PERIOD
LAST NAME	FIRST NAME TEST #	ONE	TWO	THREE	FOUR	FIVE	SIX	SEVEN	EIGHT	NINE	AVERAGE
ONE	STUDENT	100	100	100	100	100	100	100	98	100	99.7
TWO	STUDENT	33	50	37	17	67	33	50	67	67	46.7
THREE	STUDENT	100	99	100	100	100	89	95	100	100	98.1
FOUR	STUDENT	50	100	100	100	100	100	100	98	83	92.3
FIVE	STUDENT	100	100	100	100	100	100	100	100	100	100
SIX	STUDENT	83	83	100	83	67	89	100	98	100	89.2
SEVEN	STUDENT	67	83	100	100	100	95	10	98	100	93.6
EIGHT	STUDENT	100	84	100	76	84	79	73	89	85	85.5
NINE	STUDENT	100	95	94	100	94	79	100	95	97	94.8
TEN	STUDENT	85	87	95	100	90	87	90	95	95	91.5
ELEVEN	STUDENT	100	98	100	100	97	95	100	100	98	98.6
TWELVE	STUDENT	67	75	80	96	90	87	96	90	95	86.2
THIRTEEN	STUDENT	99	100	100	98	100	100	100	100	100	99.6
FOURTEEN	STUDENT	100	100	100	100	100	100	100	99	100	99.8
FIFTEEN	STUDENT	75	87	90	93	100	95	98	95	94	91.8
SIXTEEN	STUDENT	98	95	90	93	98	85	100	85	87	92.3
SEVENTEEN	STUDENT	100	95	100	87	100	85	95	99	92	94.7
EIGHTEEN	STUDENT	75	80	85	87	90	75	86	88	88	83.7
NINETEEN	STUDENT	98	100	100	100	100	100	99	100	100	99.6
TWENTY	STUDENT	75	80	87	93	95	90	90	89	90	87.6

an example, *We are working to strengthen John's written expression by having him use more details and elaboration.* Or, *In reading groups, we are focusing on having Sarah take her time with independent reading to increase her comprehension level of materials read.*

The final portion of the report card comment should be devoted to things the parents can focus on at home to help their child. For instance, *When working on written homework, have John use the webbing techniques we discussed at our last conference. Using these techniques will help to strengthen John's written work.* And, *When completing nightly reading, ask Sarah questions pertaining to the reading before she starts reading. In this way, Sarah will focus on finding the answers to the questions during the reading.*

The purpose of report card comments is to provide the parents with specific information regarding their child that will let them know how the child is doing in your classroom while giving them information that will allow them to work to improve their child's progress. Making specific comments will be much more helpful than just giving generic comments such as *Sarah is an excellent student. Keep up the good work.* Well thought-out comments will let the parents know that you truly know their child as an individual and are committed to their child's academic development.

Prior to sending report cards home, always make a copy of each report card to keep at school. In the event a child loses a report card or does not share it with his or her parent, you will have a copy on hand.

GRADING DAILY WORK

Handling and checking daily work can be an overwhelming task for beginning teachers. It is best to check as much work as you can while on school grounds. Lugging heavy book bags full of work home is not a good habit to get into.

Check as much student work as you can during the school day, while the children are present. Checking student work as it is turned in not only keeps you from having mounds of things to check later, it holds the students accountable for turning in their best work. If the students know that you will look at their work immediately upon completion, you are more likely to get quality work. This also allows you to give your students immediate, meaningful feedback about their class work as well as an opportunity for the students to make necessary corrections.

You may wish to use a checklist section of your grade book to keep track of pieces of student work that have been turned in. For nongraded items, you could simply mark a check by the student's name indicating that the child has turned in a particular assignment. Items that you feel need to be given an official grade should be entered in your grade book according to subject.

You should check all class work completed by your students. If the work is important enough for the students to do, it is important enough for you to check. Checking student work will give you valuable information regarding each individual's strengths and weaknesses in assigned areas. Use this information for future planning and formation of skills groups to help those children requiring extra assistance and practice.

Student work should be sent home at least twice a month for students and parents to review. Parents should be instructed to go over class work with their child, help the child make any necessary corrections, and sign and return the work or the folder the work was sent in as well as any comments pertaining to the class work. This is an important way of keeping parents informed regarding what is being done in the classroom and how their child is performing on assignments.

It may come to your attention that some of your students' parents are not going over class work with their children for a variety of reasons. If this is the case, you will need to take the time to go over the work with the child whose parents are unable or unwilling to do so. If you are very busy, you may assign this duty to your teaching assistant or a parent volunteer so that the child benefits from help in going over and correcting completed work.

GRADING HOMEWORK

It is not always necessary to assign grades on homework. What is necessary is to make sure students are completing assignments correctly and to your expectations. This can done quickly. Check marks can be recorded in the homework section of your grade book to indicate correct completion of homework assignments. You can select certain pieces of homework to spend extra time going over and offering feedback on.

If you have parents sign their child's homework when it is completed, most will see their child's homework, so there is no need to send homework back home. If individual children are having difficulty with homework assignments, or are completing assignments incorrectly, these assignments can be sent home with a note attached giving feedback on how to complete homework in the future. Give the child the opportunity to redo the assignment correctly.

You may have children in your classroom who do not have a great support system at home for homework. You will need to appeal to parents of children who do not complete their homework to let them know how important homework is for their child's success in school. Let these parents know how they can help their child with homework. After you have talked with the parents, if the child's homework is still not being completed, you may need to find ways to allow the child to work on essential homework activities sometime during the school day.

10

Using Technology in the Classroom

Technology has opened many windows of opportunity for today's students. Many classrooms are now equipped with computers, internet service, laser disc players, and more. Children are able to access information and work on skills in new and exciting ways. Once you have determined what is available for you and your students, you will need to get educated yourself in the many applications of the technology available. It is a terrible shame to have technology not being used, or being underused, due to teacher ignorance. Find ways through either your school, district, or local colleges to understand how to use the technology provided for you and your students.

USE OF COMPUTERS

Computers can be powerful tools. Many things are possible now through the use of computers that were unimaginable 15 years ago. Even the youngest children can be very effective in mastering computer skills. As computers continue to become more affordable, they will become more accessible to schools and school personnel.

You will find that using computers will aid in your preparing parental communications, planning, researching, creating classroom activities and materials, and opening doors for student learning.

USING THE COMPUTER AS A COMMUNICATION TOOL

As mentioned earlier, the computer can be the perfect tool for creating newsletters and other written communications to be sent home. Work completed on the computer looks more professional than handwritten communications and communications done on a typewriter. Many programs include educational clip art that will dress up your work. It will be very helpful to have a good word processing program as well as a program with a newsletter format for your communications with parents.

USING THE COMPUTER TO PLAN AND RESEARCH

The Internet is a remarkable resource. From wherever you choose to use the Internet, you can get information from all over the world. You may find yourself accessing the Internet from home, from school, or from your public library. Through use of the Internet, you will be able to access information on almost any topic in a matter of minutes. You can use the Internet to research subject matter, search libraries, find information about the authors and illustrators of books you are using in your classroom, and find free lesson plans ready for use in your classroom based upon what you are studying.

The first thing you will need to do is find Internet access. If you do not have Internet capabilities in your home, ask if you have these capabilities at school. Some schools provide Internet access in all classrooms. Others do not have Internet access in all classrooms, but might have access in a computer lab or in the media center. If you cannot access the Internet at home or at school, you can always go to the public library.

Once you have found access, you will need to find out how to use the Internet. You will need to find a support person or friend who will guide you through the basics. You may also want to check out reference guides dealing with the Internet at the public library or purchase a reference guide at your local bookstore. You will need to find out the names of several search engines to start. Search engines allow you to type in names and phrases describing what you are looking for when you don't have a specific Internet address.

When you are planning units, you can go to a search engine, type in the name of the unit, and see what you find. You will be able to find a wealth of information in a matter of minutes.

For example, say you and your students want to complete a unit about butterflies because there have been many butterflies on your campus recently. You may know of one book that you want to use. You know that *The Very Hungry Caterpillar* by Eric Carle is about a caterpillar who turns into a butterfly. Using a search engine, you type in **The Very Hungry Caterpillar by Eric Carle**. You find that more than 11,000 sites come up in response. These sites will include the official Eric Carle Web site and many others giving biographies, lesson plans, and so on. You can scan through the descriptions of the Web sites to see what appeals to you and what you think will be meaningful to your students. Through looking for this one piece of literature, you will get many ideas for your unit and links to other things to search for.

While researching this unit, you want to get information about butterflies. You go to a search engine and type **butterflies.** You find that over 600,000 sites are listed so you want to narrow the search down. You then type in **butterflies and caterpillars.** With this entered, you find about 250,000 sites. Still wanting to narrow the search, you type in **monarch butterflies and caterpillars** since this is what you and your students have decided to focus on. With this search, you get over 53,000 sites. You can further narrow your search by typing in **monarch butterflies and caterpillars in (your state).**

Many authors and illustrators of children's books have their own Web sites. Prior to completing an author study, go online to see if the author and/or illustrator you are interested in has a Web site. These Web sites often include activities for children to complete, information about the author/illustrator, ways to contact the author/illustrator, and even ways to purchase materials by the author/illustrator online.

There is an abundance of free lesson plans available online. You may come across them by searching for your subject matter. When conducting the above-mentioned search on butterflies, many lesson plans were found in the sites listed. Another way to access lesson plans is to type in **lesson plans** for whatever grade level you are interested in. You can choose the lessons and plans you are interested in using.

Be sure to take advantage of this wonderful tool. Don't let ignorance keep you from discovering how much information you can gather in a very short period of time. Find a way to access and learn how to use the Internet. Experimentation is going to be one of your best avenues to learn how to use the Internet. If you are new to the Internet, after a while you will wonder how you ever functioned without it.

USING THE COMPUTER TO DEVELOP STUDENT ACTIVITIES

As you become skilled with the computer, you will find creative ways to present information to your students and create activities for them. Often the perfect instructional activity will be the one you create. Only you know the specific needs of your students. Creators of mass-market materials do not have this information.

The following section will show teacher-made activities using the computer that were made to meet students' particular needs. The first three samples are spelling activities created by a first-grade teacher. This first-grade classroom was not assigned spelling books or a spelling curriculum, so she created her own materials and activities for spelling.

The first spelling sheet was made using a simple word processing program. The teacher chose a large and bold font to make the materials more readable for the students. The incomplete sentences were made with the students' interests in mind. For example, this particular school year, the movie *Titanic* was all anyone could talk about. The students enjoyed reading and working with sentences related to what they knew and what was familiar to them.

The second spelling practice sheet was made using a newsletter program. The teacher selected this program to have the spelling words at the top separated from the rest of the text. The teacher selected a one-column format and entered information. Again, a large and bold font was selected. This time, the teacher used the names of students in her classroom to generate interest in the material. Students love reading about themselves.

The third spelling practice sheet was created using a spreadsheet program. The teacher selected the size of the cells and the fonts to best display spelling words and letters forming spelling words on one page. The teacher wanted her children to use manipulative letters to practice forming their spelling words. This type of activity could be completed at school or at home as homework. Once students have practiced forming spelling words several times, the letters could be glued onto a piece of construction or other paper to form spelling words and be turned in to the teacher.

Spelling Practice Sheet 1

Use the words below to fill in the blanks of the sentences.

| she | sheep | should |
| shop | ship | shape |

1. The Titanic was a very large _____.

2. _____ is my best friend.

3. Sometimes a cloud can look like a _____.

4. I like to _____ at the store.

5. A square is a _____ that has four sides.

6. You _____ read every night.

Spelling Practice Sheet 2

Directions: Use your spelling words to fill in the blanks.

play	plays	played	playing
jump	jumps	jumped	jumping

1. Jamar is _____ with Angelo.

2. Will you _____ with me?

3. Lauren likes to _____ on her bed.

4. John and Andy are _____ up and down.

5. Yesterday, Naquella _____ with Erica.

6. Payton _____ and runs when he plays soccer.

Spelling Practice Sheet 3

Directions: Cut out each rectangle. Form each spelling word using individual letters.

she	sheep	should	shop
	shape	ship	
h	o	s	p
h	d	h	o
p	i	s	i
a	s	u	h
p	e	e	p
h	s	e	s
s	h	e	h

The next three teacher-made activities were designed for phonics and language arts. Each of these activities was created using a newsletter format and program. The teacher selected the desired number of columns and typed in the needed information.

The first activity was created as an assessment for student mastery in word families the students had been working with in class. The students were to write words belonging to each word family in the appropriate column. The teacher could easily determine, after the completion of the activity, which students had a thorough understanding of the word families.

In the second activity, students cut out words from the word sheet and placed them in the appropriate column by sorting the words into base words, words ending with **-s**, words ending with **-ed**, and words ending with **-ing**. The words were typed using a spreadsheet program. The teacher was careful to compare the size of the cells to make sure they would fit in the designated columns.

The third activity was a review activity for students of the short vowel sounds **a, e,** and **i**. Students in this classroom enjoyed completing magazine searches for pictures and words. The teacher used this interest to develop the review activity. This type of activity could be completed by all students or placed in a center for a few students at a time to work on.

Phonics and Language Arts Activity 1

Short a Word Families		
-an	-ack	-at

Phonics and Language Arts Activity 2

Paste each of the words in the correct column.		
playing	hopes	played
jumped	hop	skip
hopping	jump	plays
hops	hopped	skips
skipping	jumps	play
hope	hoping	jumping
	hoped	skipped

Word Endings			
base word	*-s*	*-ed*	*-ing*

Look through magazines. Glue pictures or words containing each of the vowel sounds below.		
short a	short e	short i

The following two activities are based upon the story *D. W. All Wet* by Marc Brown. These activities were designed for a reading group needing extra work with contractions. The students in this classroom were doing an author study of the works of Marc Brown. The teacher found a Marc Brown story containing many contractions for the reading group needing this type of reinforcement.

The first activity was typed using a word processing program. The cut-and-paste activity was created using a spreadsheet program. For this activity, students were directed to cut out the word cards and match the contraction to the two words making up each contraction.

Contraction Activity 1*: *D. W. All Wet* by Marc Brown

Write the two words for each contraction.

1. "*It's* too hot?" shouted D.W.

_____   _____

2. "*That's* why we came to the beach," said Mother.

_____   _____

3. I *"don't* like the beach," said D.W.

_____   _____

4. "And I *don't* like to get wet."

_____   _____

5. *"Here's* a good spot," said Father.

_____   _____

6. *"I'm* not playing," said D.W.

_____   _____

7. "I *don't* want to get sunburned."

_____   _____

8. "I *don't* like the water."

_____   _____

9. "You *haven't* even tried it,"
   said Father.

_____   _____

10. *"I'm* going for a walk."

_____   _____

11. "You walk. *I'll* ride."

_____   _____

12. "But I *can't* see!" said Arthur.

_____   _____

Contraction Activity 2*

Cut out the word cards and match the contraction to the two words that make up each contraction. Use with *D. W. All Wet* by Marc Brown.

It's	Here is
That's	I am
Don't	Do not
Here's	Have not
I'm	That is
Haven't	Can not
Can't	It is
I'll	I will

These samples show several different possibilities for using computers and computer programs to design activities to meet the needs of the students in your classroom. Although these activities were designed for language arts, activities can as easily be designed for science, math, social studies, and other areas. Once you begin working with the computer and designing activities for your students, you will begin to see more possibilities for creating meaningful, fun activities for your class.

*SOURCE: The two contraction activities are from D. W. All Wet by Marc Brown. Copyright © 1987 by Marc Brown. Reprinted by permission of Little, Brown and Company, Inc.

STUDENT USE OF COMPUTERS

There are many programs designed for school-aged children available on the market today. There are literature-based programs, word processing programs, child encyclopedia programs, and programs designed for special interests. You will find a wide range of programs suitable for children in the age group you are teaching.

Your school may provide a variety of software for your classroom. You may also wish to invest in software to enhance your academic program, using either school funds or your own money. Become knowledgeable about what type of software is compatible with the computers in your school. You may wish to write down the necessary specifications so you will be able to refer to them when you look at software.

It is best, if you get a chance, to preview software before purchasing. Most places selling software do not accept returns of opened boxes. If you have already seen the software in action and have used your list of specifications to ensure that the software will work on your computers, you will not get stuck with software that will not meet your needs.

USE OF PHOTOGRAPHY IN THE CLASSROOM

There are many uses for photography in the classroom. It is a worthwhile investment to have both a standard camera and an instant camera in your classroom at all times. Photographs can be used for specific lessons, for discipline purposes, and for special projects.

As mentioned previously, make sure to get parent permission at the beginning of the school year to photograph children in your classroom. Be sure to keep these signed permission forms in a safe, secure place.

You will need to let your lessons be your guide as to how to use photography in the classroom. For example, if you were working with writing descriptive paragraphs with primary students, you could take pictures of very identifiable people and objects in your school. You might take a picture of the school cafeteria, the principal, a globe in your classroom, and the playground. You could have your students work in cooperative groups. Each group could write to describe the photograph presented without naming the person, place, or thing. Your students could read their descriptions to the remainder of the class. The remaining students would use the descriptions to try to identify the person, place, or thing depicted in the photograph.

In a classroom working on identifying geometric solids, students could be armed with instant cameras and go on a scavenger hunt for geometric solids located on their school grounds. Students could photograph balls for spheres, ice cream cones for cones, and wooden blocks as examples of rectangular prisms. Once students found suitable items to photograph, these photographs could be shared in the classroom and used to make a class graph of the examples of geometric solids found on the school campus.

Many times, just having an instant camera will aid in your classroom discipline. Students in primary grades often try to test the limits. When you see undesirable behavior such as sulking, tantruming, or blatant refusal to do work, simply get out your instant camera and let the student know that you are going to take a picture to send home to his or her parents. In 99% of these situations, the undesirable behavior will immediately cease without your ever having to take a picture.

In the case of a child experiencing severe discipline problems, photographs you take of the child's inappropriate behaviors can serve as documentation for your behavioral documentation log. Make sure to write the date, time, and a brief note of the circumstances leading up to the inappropriate behaviors and how you dealt with them. Place photographs with other documentation in the child's behavior log.

Photographs can be used for many special projects in the classroom. At the beginning of the year, you may wish to take pictures of all of your students and make copies of them for use throughout the school year. You can fasten student pictures to completed work to display in your classroom. You can use these pictures on special art projects. Student pictures could be used as illustrations of characters in class-made books.

The possibilities for using photography in the classroom are endless. Use your imagination and the imagination of your students to see where photography can lead you. Your students will truly enjoy this visual, stimulating approach to learning.

Photography can be a fairly expensive endeavor. Instant photography is especially costly. In your letters to parents, express that donations of instant film or other needed types of film would be greatly appreciated. If you explain to parents how you plan to use the film, many will be willing to donate film for your classroom purposes.

11

Planning for Special Events

Teaching often includes duties that go beyond or enhance the curriculum. Each year, you will more than likely be responsible for providing classroom parties for your students at certain times of the school year. You will also probably participate in planning for and supervising at least one field trip per year for your class. Below are suggestions for planning for these events, recruiting volunteers to help with these events, and tips for adequately supervising these special events.

CLASS PARTIES

In the primary grades, classroom parties are often expected at certain times of the year. Holidays are times when classroom parties may be allowed and even expected. Check your school guidelines regarding classroom parties. Your school may even designate certain times and dates for classroom parties.

Classroom parties will require a great deal of planning on your part to run smoothly. Students who are used to your regular classroom routine and structure may have difficulty dealing with an unstructured time. Classroom parties can be planned simply or more extravagantly. It will be up to you to decide what type of party to plan for your students.

The simplest type of party is to provide a special snack for your students. The snack can be provided by a volunteering parent or by you. During your classroom party, students will be able to enjoy their snacks and socialize quietly with each other.

More extravagant parties can be conducted in a learning center atmosphere. In order to have a center party, you will need the help of several parent volunteers. You will need to meet with these volunteers prior to the party to plan activities and decide what materials will be needed for the party. By planning prior to the event, you will be sure that all will run smoothly.

For example, you and several of your parents are working together to plan a party prior to the winter holidays. You want to have centers for the children to work in for their party. The centers you plan need to be appropriate for all of the children in your classroom. If completing holiday activities, make sure to have activities representative of the holidays celebrated by your children. For example, depending on the makeup of your class, you may wish to have Kwanzaa, Christmas, and Hanukkah activities at your party. For example, you have 25 students in your classroom. You and the parents decide that you would like to have five children working in each center. Therefore, you will need to have five center activities.

For the first center, you have decided you would like the children to make a holiday card for someone in their family. You will need to have materials for making the cards, such as construction paper, markers, glue, and stickers.

In the second center, students will use icing to decorate holiday cookies. The children will then eat their cookies. Supplies needed for this activity will be cups, napkins, cookies, icing, and juice to have with the cookies.

The third center, you have decided, will be an art activity. Students will make a holiday wreath. Materials needed for this center will be a ready-made wreath form, decorative materials to glue onto the wreath, and glue.

The fourth center will be a listening center. The parent who runs this center will read holiday stories to the children. Materials for this center will be holiday stories.

The final center will be a center where children can decorate a paper bag using holiday stickers and other appropriate items. Materials needed for this center will be bags, stickers, construction paper, glue, and scissors. After the party, the children can use these bags to transport their holiday party goodies home.

During the party, you will rotate the children through the five centers. It is best if you have a parent to run each center. In this way, you will be free to maintain order and oversee the party. You will need to time each center so that each center activity runs from 10 to 15 minutes. All children will need to stay in the designated center until asked to rotate to the next center. It is helpful to set a timer as each center activity begins so that you can keep things running in the timed intervals that you have planned for.

Determine, ahead of time, how much time you will need to designate for the classroom party to allow all students to participate in each center. Allow extra time in case your activities run over. If your classroom party is at the end of the day, it is helpful to have the children pack to go home before the party begins. This will be one less thing you will have to worry about at the end of the day.

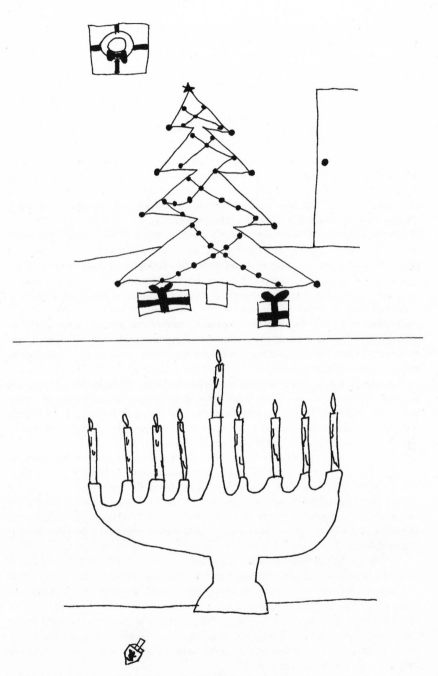

Samples of Student Illustrations for Holiday Cards

Always be sure to thank volunteering parents for their time and efforts. Class parties run much more smoothly with parental help. If planned properly, everyone should enjoy your classroom party!

FIELD TRIPS

Field trips are always greatly anticipated by students. Your field trips should always be based on your curriculum. Once you have selected a trip experience to tie into the curriculum, you will need to do all you can to ensure a safe, fun field trip. Often, you will not have as much control over a field trip experience as over a classroom experience. Always expect the unexpected.

You will need to do several things prior to field trip day. First, you will need to ask for volunteers to help chaperon. Extra hands are a necessity for field trips. It would be nice if you could have one adult per five children for your field trip. Find out in advance if chaperons must pay a fee. Communicate this information to potential volunteers from the beginning. Most volunteers will not mind paying admission for field trips as long as they have this information from the start. Let the parents know that they will be assigned a group of children and responsible for the supervision of that group throughout the class trip. If at all possible, try to get two or three parents as substitutes in case some of your chaperons are unable to come at the last minute.

Check to see how lunch will be handled on the day of the field trip. If you will be away from campus during lunch time, determine procedures for ordering lunches from the cafeteria or send letters home asking parents to provide children with sack lunches. Ask a teacher who taught at your school last year about the handling of lunch procedures or ask your cafeteria manager.

Prior to the day of the field trip, find out all you can about what the trip consists of. If the trip is to someplace local, you may even wish to visit the field trip destination on your own before you go with your students. By doing this, you will be more knowledgeable about how to guide your students through activities and be able to foresee potential problems for your students. If a visit is not convenient, call the place you will be visiting and ask for information regarding the program for your students.

On the day of the field trip, have name tags ready for all students and adults. It might be helpful to provide different types of name tags for each group. One adult will have all the children with apple-shaped name tags, another adult will have all of the children with pencil-shaped name tags, and so on. Provide each adult with a list of students he or she is in charge of. When assigning students to adults, make sure to put the adult's child in his or her group. Also, be sure children with behavior problems are spread out among the group. Children with the most severe behaviors should be in your group.

When leaving for your field trip, you will need to have a piece of paper with all of your students' names on it. Include an emergency contact number for each child. Several times during the trip, call the roll to make sure all children are accounted for. This will be extremely important when leaving the trip destination to head back to school. It is your responsibility that all children are safe and accounted for at all times. Your chaperons will assist with this, but you are the responsible party.

You may wish to pack a small book bag with items such as baby wipes, safety pins, antibacterial hand gel, a first aid kit, and so on, to take along on the trip. Often it is difficult to find accommodations for hand washing for your students prior to lunch on field trips. If possible, take a cellular phone with you so you can communicate with your school or parents in emergency situations. Your supplies will make for a more pleasant outing.

The time you take to prepare for your trip will make for a more enjoyable, smoothly run experience for you, your students, and your chaperons. Be prepared.

12

Professionalism of Teaching

You have chosen a very rewarding profession. You will need to act like the professional you are in all aspects of your day-to-day performance. This chapter will focus on how to develop positive relationships with others, the importance of getting involved in school committees, the benefits of joining a professional organization, and the importance of creating and maintaining a professional portfolio.

RELATIONSHIPS WITH OTHERS

In today's society, teachers tend to be viewed very critically. There is not much status in being an educator. You will need to make a positive effort to carry yourself as the professional you are at all times. Always be sure to act in a professional manner while dealing with students, parents, colleagues, and administrators.

At times, dealing with young students can become frustrating. No matter how frustrated you might become, never let the students sense your frustration. Do not ever yell at your students. Once you become a "screamer," you have lost the battle. Students know when they have gotten to a teacher. It is good advice to act as if you are being observed at all times. You would not ever act inappropriately during an observation. If you always behave in the manner in which you would conduct yourself during an observation, you will always treat children in the positive manner they deserve. Disciplining children can always be done while maintaining both your professionalism and the students' dignity.

Parents can be very powerful forces at your school. Always deal with parents, even those who can occasionally become unreasonable, in a confident, fair manner. Parents need to know that you are a knowledgeable and caring individual. Parents will always talk to one another. You will earn a reputation at your school. Do all you can to earn a positive reputation. Parents will specifically ask for teachers with good reputations. You will want your name on this list.

Teaching sometimes feels fairly isolated since, for the most part, you are the only adult or one of the only adults in a classroom for most of the day. Use times when you are not with your children to get to know your colleagues. Your working atmosphere will be much more pleasant if you have others to turn to for advice, others' help with difficult situations, and others' friendship. Do not limit these positive interactions to the teachers. You should get to know and develop positive relationships with all adults at your school. People are much more likely to help you in a time of need if you have been courteous and friendly throughout the school year.

Your administrators will be a big part of your job satisfaction. It is extremely important to develop and maintain a positive rapport with your administrators. One of the best ways to do this is always to keep your administrators informed. A simple way to keep them informed is by providing them with a copy of your newsletter each week. Your newsletter will give your administrative team important information regarding your instructional program. If you ever have situations arise that you are not comfortable with, make sure to let your administrative team know about these situations. Administrators would rather know of possible conflicts from you ahead of time, than be stampeded by parents without prior warning. Part of your administrators' job is to be instructional leaders and to help teachers. Seek their help when necessary.

GETTING INVOLVED WITH SCHOOL COMMITTEES

One way to continue to grow as a professional is to get involved and serve on various committees in your school. By working on committees you will learn more about your school and school community. You will also be involved in the decision-making process at your school. If you are new to a school, ask what types of committees the school has. Let your administrators know that you would be interested in serving on one of the committees.

GETTING INVOLVED WITH PROFESSIONAL ORGANIZATIONS

Once you have secured your teaching position, one of the first things you will need to do is join a professional organization. There are professional organizations on the national, state, and local levels. Most professional organizations require that you pay dues. This may seem like a lot of money at first, but membership is an absolute necessity. Find out from colleagues and administrators about the professional organizations for your area as soon as possible. You may also refer to the Internet to research national, state, and local professional organizations and their benefits to members.

Professional organizations help keep you informed about your profession while providing you with other valuable services. One of the services that can be gained through professional organizations is legal aid. Unfortunately, we live in a society that likes to sue. Even the most outstanding teachers can be wrongfully accused of wrongdoing. Being a member of a professional organization is like carrying an insurance policy. These organizations will aid with legal expenses in the event that this service is needed.

Professional organizations provide teachers with valuable information through newsletters. These newsletters provide members with information about the educational organization and about current trends in education. Some professional organizations now even have their own Web sites.

Other benefits professional organizations provide for their members may include: insurance programs and special rates, advice about saving and investing, lower rates on credit cards, and discount programs for other desired services.

Look into your professional organization options. Look into the benefits these organizations provide. Once you have weighed the options, join the professional organization that is right for you.

CREATING A PROFESSIONAL PORTFOLIO

As you are growing as a professional, you will need to create a professional portfolio. A professional portfolio is a tremendous asset for gaining both initial and transfer employment. An impressive portfolio will let your future employer know that you are well organized. The contents of the portfolio should be items that you have selected to present the best picture possible of your professional career and qualifications. After looking at your portfolio, you want a future employer to think, "Yes, this is the right person for this job!"

You can begin working on putting together a professional portfolio right away. Your portfolio should contain documentation of your teaching career. You may include such items as school transcripts, letters of recommendation, evaluations, and photographs depicting your classroom environment.

Photographs really dress up a professional portfolio. Throughout the school year, take pictures of exciting activities that you and your students engage in. Take pictures of student work that you have displayed and of the classroom environment in general. The pictures will provide an attractive display of your talents.

Portfolio contents should be placed in an attractive, durable binder. Keep in mind that you will need to be able to add things to and remove things from the portfolio as your career progresses. One suggestion is to find an attractive, perhaps leather, three-ring binder for your portfolio. All of your portfolio contents could be placed in sheet protectors before placing them in the binder. The sheet protectors will keep your items in good shape and provide an easy method for adding and discarding portfolio contents.

Your portfolio should be regularly maintained and updated. You might have an unexpected opportunity arise. If your portfolio is always ready for an interview, so are you.

As an addition to your portfolio, you might wish to include a videotape highlighting special works you have done with children. The video should be short, highlight your best work, and present a variety of different activities. You could fairly inexpensively make copies of the video to leave with prospective employers.

However you choose to do your professional portfolio, make your portfolio show what you want employers to see about you as a professional. Always keep your portfolio updated and improved. You will benefit greatly from the time you put into making your portfolio.

CONCLUSION

Your years of teaching will be an exciting journey. Your individual teaching style and beliefs will change over the years. I am a completely different teacher today as I enter my fourteenth year teaching in the primary grades than I was during my first few years of teaching. My style of teaching has been shaped by all of the wonderful students, colleagues, and administrators I have had the opportunity to work with. My teaching techniques have changed as I have continued to take courses and read great books and magazines about my profession.

You have just started on this exciting journey. I hope that the ideas in this book will be valuable tools to take on that journey. You can choose the ideas you like and modify ideas as you continue to search for your individual style. My wish for you is that your career as a teacher will be as rewarding as mine has been.

Index